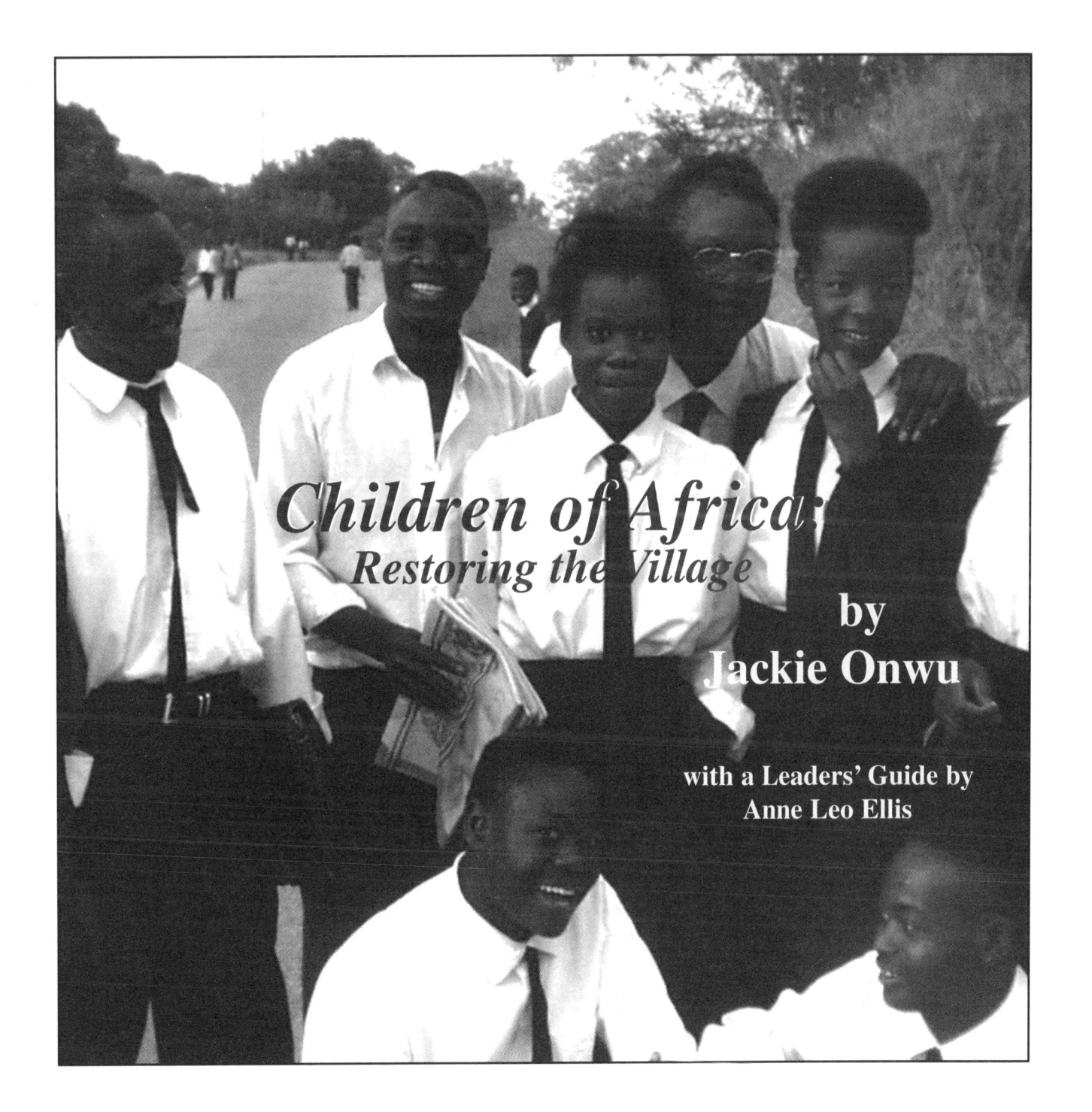

Children of Africa:
Restoring the Village

by
Jackie Onwu

with a Leaders' Guide by
Anne Leo Ellis

Children of Africa: Restoring the Village
Copyright, 2000 General Board of Global Ministries

A publication of
the General Board of Global Ministries
The United Methodist Church

Cover design: Edward A. Moultrie
Photos: Lesley Y. Crosson
ISBN# 1-890569-28-3

All biblical quotations, unless otherwise noted, are from the New Revised Standard Version (NRSV) of the Bible, copyright© 1989 by the Division of Christian Education of the National Council of the Churches of Christ in the United States of America. Used by permission. All rights reserved.

Contents

Preface

Introduction   iv

World of the African Child   vi

1. Children's Health: A Dearth of Good Care   1

2. Children's Education: A Lack of Good Schooling   13

3. Armed Conflict and the Destruction of Childhood   21

4. The Shattered Lives of Forgotten Children   31

5. Decisions of Nations: Their Impact on Children   43

6. The Church in Africa: Source of Caring, Courage, and Hope   55

7. We Are All Part of the Global Village   61

Appendices

Glossary

End Notes

Resources

Preface

A Statement about the Bishops' Appeal, Hope for the Children of Africa

Children are meant to be happy; yet for many, the detours to that goal are a shambles of disease, poverty, and violence. Our children in Africa, longing for joy, are traveling the roads leading to tragic sadness. The United Methodist Church weeps for those who weep in Africa, and our tears must take the form of gifts of compassion.

Hope for the Children of Africa will rebuild caring structures that have been devastated by war. *Hope for the Children of Africa* will create renewed and new ministries sharing the gospel of Jesus Christ to give hope. *Hope for the Children of Africa* will address the horrors of war, advance peace, and provide caring communities, where children can be "at home."

We call upon our churches to celebrate the faith and hope of our children in Africa. May we go to the children of Africa, so they can hear the stories of Jesus and experience his welcoming love. When God's children become our children, hope will abound!

Robert Morgan, president, Council of Bishops, The United Methodist Church
George W. Bashore, past president, Council of Bishops, The United Methodist Church

Introduction

The sound of Africa is not just the sound of war. It is the sound of children playing and laughing. It is the sound of people singing God's praise. It is the sound of hope. The children have hope and we have hope because we trust in Him who won the victory at Calvary. We believe that one day we will overcome these difficulties. That is why we cannot stop educating the children and caring for them. It is why we must stand together to nurture this faith and hope that lives in our children. And, as a church we cannot wait, we must do it now.

— Bishop J. Alfred Ndoricimpa, East Africa Annual Conference

Unfortunately, many Americans have a very different perception of Africa. This is based largely on media presentations that are informative but tend to play on our emotions rather than help us become sensitive to the issues. Thus, we are alarmed by reports of war and revolution, corruption, and a losing battle for development. We are saddened by the sunken faces and swollen bellies of children engulfed by famine; made fearful by the reality of sundry atrocities. These responses, though legitimate, often cause us to miss the real issue: behind all the vivid depictions, there are individuals like ourselves who must conduct their daily lives in circumstances most of us find unimaginable. There are children who, through no fault of their own, are victims—impoverished, uneducated, and with their rights, their health, even their lives, at risk.

Children are the first to succumb to wars, famine, disease, and natural disasters. They are also the first to be victimized by the physical and moral decadence of their societies. Throughout much of Africa, theirs is a world in which the term "childhood" (the state or period of being a child) has little to do with a pre-adult period of preparation and learning, as well as of untroubled play. Currently, prevailing political, social, and economic factors throughout the continent mean that vast numbers of African children—defined by their young years—have no childhood to enjoy.

We begin this study with a look at the starkness of life for many contemporary African children. In the first chapter we examine the lack of basic health care for children who may suffer from malnutrition, AIDS, lack of clean water, and absence of the most rudimentary medical care. Chapter 2 looks at education, or, rather the lack of it for the greatest number of African children. The third chapter discusses the devastation that the wars of Africa have caused for its children, including the scourges of child soldiers and the sexual exploitation of children. Chapter 4 examines child labor, the lives of street children, and the reality of slavery, even in our own day. Throughout the book, but especially in chapter 5, we examine the politics and economic policies that have been fundamental in creating the present social environment of children in Africa. Chapter 6 discusses the faith, courage, and caring of African Christians and the African church. And, finally, in chapter 7, we learn about some of The United Methodist Church's projects and programs—developed by U.S. annual conferences and African central conferences and local churches—to increase the quality of life and assure a more rewarding future for many of Africa's young people.

Given the vastness of the continent, many issues cannot be addressed in this book. Furthermore, in order to focus on problems in regions with central conference relationships, more attention has been given to sub-Saharan Africa than to the countries in the north, except when addressed within the framework of international organizations such as the United Nations. A great effort has been made to avoid using the term "African" as a convenient label for any phenomenon occurring on the continent. Generalizations are used only to point out similarities of cultures, histories, and events.

It is our hope that you will find this study enlightening, informative, and a source of inspiration for ways of responding in this time of crisis. As part of the global village, we, too, can contribute as the churches and other groups struggle to address some of the grim realities shaping the world of many children in Africa.

World of the African Child

The African child has always been ensured a safe and secure existence. The foundation for this security is a basic belief that children are unique beings endowed with special qualities based on God's divine order. In Africa, children are believed to be very close to God, lent to parents, but still under God's watchful eye, and engaged in a relationship with God that is different from their relationship with adults. They were part of their families before they were born, since it is believed that the attributes of loved ones who have left this life will be regenerated in new individuals.

As community life retained and constantly reshaped the modes and morals of public behavior, everyone in the family and the village was responsible for the upbringing of the children. Nurturing abounded in acts of love, patience, and kindness designed to foster an environment friendly and responsive to the development of well-brought-up and well-disciplined children. Everyone in the community strove to make each individual child achieve maximum potential in an area of its own capacities and inclinations, because individual achievements were also communal achievements.

So dear are children to the heart of the African family, that in nearly all African nations children are considered wealth: "Blessed is the man that has his quiver full" (Ps. 127:5a). In other words, wealthy is the man who has many children, for he is assured of his family's continuance, of communal respect and pride as they live accomplished lives, and of his own security in old age.

This basic premise about the importance of children in African societies has not changed. However, as the societies themselves have changed—thrown into disarray by wars, famines, chaos, and inadequate systems of governance—established means to these long-cherished ends for children have all but disappeared.

This explains the fact that children are still desired even under and in spite of extreme political, economic, social, and environmental conditions. Marriages are still not complete without children, and as parents grow old in societies without a social safety net to provide such services as social security, medicare, and welfare schemes, their importance in the lives of families cannot be overestimated. They are not to be denied their entry into the world, because their mission—their heritage—is from God.

We must do all we can to make sure that Africa's children are given every opportunity—even in the face of scant resources and unwelcoming environments—to fulfill their God-ordained purpose in this life.

1
Children's Health: A Dearth of Good Care

Today I visited a hospital. I can't describe it—so dingy, everything brown or green. Hospitals are supposed to be white! Clean! But not here. The beds were so old and rusty, with no mattresses on them. There was no smell of ether or alcohol or disinfectant. Only the smell of urine and vomit. No toilets! No water! No electricity! No medicines! Too many broken windows.

Many people were lying out on the walkway, trying to escape the heat. They had TB. The sanitarium is too far and too expensive, so they stay here. A beautiful young girl sat on the veranda. She had a hole in her leg, all the way through the bone. She had been there for a year—waiting! She's going to lose the leg, I was told, because there is no medicine. All they can do for her is wash it. They just wash it with water from the stream each day. I asked her how she felt. She told me she hadn't eaten for two days. Then I heard a baby crying. He's going to die—maybe tomorrow, they said. The family cannot afford to pay for the consultation. These types of cases are cared for by a nurse. The nurse is inexperienced and can't even operate, they tell me . . .

The baby died today. Tonight the funeral drums are beating in three different directions. Lord God, I thank you for allowing me to be here, but this place is tough!

———— Onwu, *The Diary of a Missionary,* an unpublished work

A Dearth of Good Health Care

The fiscal crunch facing nearly all African countries has taken its toll on health care—both its delivery and its facilities. Most government health care facilities were built during the colonial period. Today they are inadequate, weather-worn, and in disrepair. The population booms early in the post-independence era quickly outpaced the capabilities of existing health care systems. Some countries were able to build new facilities and expand the number of teaching hospitals, but it is not happening fast enough to keep up with public demand. In the meantime, everyone suffers—and, most unjustly, innocent children.

Under the United Nations' Convention on the Rights of the Child, children have a right to the highest attainable standard of health care (Article 24). The convention recognizes that not all governments have the necessary resources, but it commits them to take it seriously, and to ensure the best use of available resources. Since the beginning of the economic downturn in the late '70s and early '80s, health care, which was already overburdened, has suffered consistent cuts. In 1996, sub-Saharan Africa as a region spent as much on debt repayment as on health care and education combined: $12 billion.

Most governments simply passed on the cost of care by no longer providing basic necessities such as drugs, syringes, bandages, intravenous drips, sterilizing solutions, and the like. These items must be purchased either at a government pharmacy or at private pharmacies in the community.

Personal Observation

[In] hospitals and health care institutions . . . there may not be such basics as water and electricity, as the economic goals of governments supercede the needs of the poor and marginalized who must depend on government services. Many die since family members cannot afford the drugs and other necessities for surgery and other treatment. Pharmacy shelves become empty or stocked with fake drugs as the foreign exchange for the purchase of quality drugs is not available. This was brought home to us with the purchase of a fake liquid antibiotic for my then two-year-old son. The more he took of the medicine, the worse he became. Finally we took him back to the doctor, who identified the medication as fake. It was bought from a reputable pharmacy, but it was fake!

For the poor, the government hospital may be the only source of primary and secondary health care. Some states have set up clinics and/or dispensaries in rural areas, but all are under-equipped and under-staffed. Many lack beds, mattresses, equipment, electricity, and water. Pharmacy shelves are empty, and sanitation is at its lowest level. With so little money being put into health care budgets, teaching hospitals have been unable to maintain the standards necessary for the training of qualified personnel. Corruption in the selection process, as well as a lowering of educational standards have both left their mark. Furthermore, throughout Africa the salaries of doctors in government institutions have declined in real terms.

It is not unusual for a health care worker or even a student to see patients privately—in offices or in the person's home—to supplement their income. This is especially true of nurses and pharmacists, on whom poor people have come to rely believing that these people know as much as doctors and are more approachable as well as cheaper. Nearly all pharmacies in the poorer areas have a small room in the back where injections are given—especially certain malaria cures—and minor surgical procedures are performed. This is how most poor people receive health care. It goes without saying that it is risky and that many lives have been unnecessarily lost.

Medical testing has fallen to the same levels. The labs in government hospitals rarely have the necessary reagents for performing reliable diagnostic tests. Private labs have sprung up everywhere. Regulations as to what training is required to perform such services are loose, and if a license is needed at all, bribery is a clear option. Although some of the personnel in these labs may be receiving training, the majority has never been properly trained. And without a qualified lab technician, even if both reagents and equipment are in place (which is frequently not the case), test accuracy is not possible.

Lack of Medical Facilities and Supplies

There may be no electricity in these labs, or, in the event of power failure, generators may be lacking. Thus, it will be impossible to keep the samples fresh. There may be problems with clean water and proper sterilization methods. In unscrupulous laboratories, no matter what the required test, no matter how many different patients, the results will be the same for all. Example: pain in the foot = malaria; upset stomach = malaria; chest pain = malaria. There are, of course, very good labs that give excellent results, but the poor cannot afford their services.

In some places, when surgery is required all the necessary medical supplies plus the doctor's fee must be paid for before bringing the patient to the hospital. It may take months to accumulate everything, including food for the patient and the person who will be in attendance. Nursing staff as we know it is hard to come by in African government hospitals. Thus family members or friends must come to the hospital with the patients, and stay to care and cook for them. When a child is hospitalized, the mother will always leave everything—even other small children—to stay at the hospital until the child is able to leave. Since few medical facilities accept payment in kind, many patients from rural areas die before all the arrangements can be made. This affects the urban poor as well.

Throughout sub-Saharan Africa, many government hospitals—the only source of health care for thousands of UMC members—lack the most basic necessities such as water, and are often without electricity due to blackouts caused by the overloading/overuse of antiquated equipment. Ironically, in 1998 the government hospital in Taraba State, Nigeria (the seat of the UMC) was upgraded to a "specialist hospital" and was called one of the country's "baby-friendly" institutions. Despite such honors, the hospital has no water and suffers from continuing power failures, low sanitary conditions, and lack of staff. In varying degrees, this is a general problem for government institutions throughout Africa.

Politics as a Negative Influence

It is unfortunate that the acquisition of drugs and other materials used in the health care sector, as well as staffing, are handled in the political realm. Politicians are either the actual purchasers or ministers (political appointees) under departments of health. The result is significant mismanagement and a lack of services to the poor. In many countries these persons have been accused of purchasing expired or fake drugs, or inadequate quantities, placing the poor at risk.

All over Africa there is a brain drain of qualified doctors. Some go into private practice, opening their own clinics, hospitals, and maternity facilities. Others are drawn overseas. Many of those educated abroad decide to remain there. Some governments do try to lure their doctors back home, and many do return. However, the frustration of government bureaucracy, poor working conditions, and low salary, as well as the nonchalant attitude about the suffering poor, have caused many doctors to throw in the towel.

Some Positive Steps

For many governments, improvements in health care translate into the creation of additional dispensaries, clinics, and hospitals. However, significant improvements can often be made by modifying the existing physical and social environments. Examples: 1. providing clean sources of water, be they boreholes, wells, or taps, and sewage and waste management facilities; 2. eliminating overcrowding and unsanitary environmental conditions; 3. controlling toxic chemical emissions and air pollution, in light of the use of diesel and other fuels; 4. immunizing children against infectious diseases.

The World Health Organization (WHO) has established a "Healthy Cities Program," aimed at promoting urban health, especially in low-income populations throughout the world. This led to World Health Day, through which all participating cities have the opportunity to demonstrate what they have achieved.

AIDS

Each day 5,500 funeral ceremonies are conducted as a result of AIDS. "And the worst is yet to come," predicts Agathe Lartre-Gato Lawson, the United Nations AIDS (UNAIDS) representative for the Ivory Coast.

——— *Le Figaro,* Paris, Nov. 25, 1998

At 57, the widowed Akwatura is raising seven young children orphaned by AIDS, four of them her own grandchildren and three others—two one-year-olds and a two-year-old—abandoned and suffering from malnutrition. "I am proud to be able to look after these orphans," Akwatura says. "I can feed them properly and I am pleased that the older ones are going to school and doing well."

——— Andrew Meldrum, Guardian News Service, London, in World Press Review, Nov., 1997, p. 42.

The AIDS virus has reached epidemic proportions in Africa, leaving in its wake devastated villages, decimated families, and tens of thousands of orphans. It is by far the most serious threat to human life on the continent, especially in sub-Saharan Africa where it has had its worst impact.

A little over ten years ago, WHO estimated that there were 130,000 cases of HIV on the whole planet, with 80,000 of them in the United States. The estimates for Africa were a mere 21,000 official cases. Today, AIDS has caused more than 12 million deaths, with 21 million on the African continent infected with the virus. To make matters even worse, 90 percent of those carrying the virus do not know they are infected, and have little idea of the potential for passing it on to others.

Throughout Africa, the initial reaction to the original statistics was denial, backed by official statements that the estimates were an attempt by the West to destabilize Africa through the use of negative propaganda. When cases of infection were found, they received little attention or sympathy because AIDS was thought to be related to homosexuality—regarded in Africa as a perversion. When the general population began to be infected, AIDS was put into the category of malaria or diabetes—that is, chronic but manageable. This view was especially taken by countries with large tourist industries. Thus, the attitudes of governments, the prevailing economic situations, and the sexual taboos associated with the virus contributed greatly to its spread. With the focus on revenue losses as well as a sense of shame surrounding the victims, no one did anything, and by the time it could no longer be ignored, AIDS had become a scourge.

In Botswana and Zimbabwe, HIV now infects more than one in four adults. In some African cities, infection rates are higher than thirty percent. WHO reports that as many as 70 percent of women attending certain African prenatal clinics are HIV-positive. South African statistics indicate that 1,500 people are infected daily, with one-third of the babies born at a Soweto hospital HIV-positive.

It is suggested that twenty percent of the country's working population may be HIV-positive by the year 2000. This is the scenario, though in varying degrees, all over sub-Saharan Africa. With the disease's principal victims between the ages of 15 and 25, African governments will need to contend with a loss of up to thirty percent of their work force in the next decade.

The Effect of Armed Conflicts

Africa's armed conflicts in recent years have also contributed to the spread of the disease. Among men in the military, because of their prevailing life style, the degree of HIV is widespread. By force, consent, or through malice because they know they are infected, soldiers aid in the spread of the virus. In situations of extreme vulnerability, where individuals are being controlled, such as in the refugee camps, the virus spreads quickly. "According to the Belgian publication *Le Soir*, the rate of HIV-positive cases in Rwandan refugee camps grew six-fold during the two years that the refugees were in Zaire."

It has been extremely difficult to curb the spread of AIDS. The reasons are several: 1. As mentioned earlier, fear and ignorance oblige victims to keep silent about their condition. 2. Low levels of literacy, coupled with taboos about the discussion of sex, hinder publication and awareness; 3. Migrant labor, wars, and unstable living conditions foster the sexual exploitation of women and children—boys as well as girls. Add to these the scourges of famine, poverty, lack of sanitation and health care, and the seeming inability of governments to address the problem adequately. Government hospitals and health care services cannot afford AZT and other drugs for treating the disease. As discussed above, they cannot even afford generic drugs for treating simple ailments. As a result, entire families have been affected, both young and old.

Children and AIDS

Children are especially endangered by AIDS. Their entire world is being changed by the disease, and they all run the risk of being infected with or affected by it. In 1997, the United Nations warned that Africa was in danger of becoming a continent of orphans unless something was done to control the spread of AIDS. At the time, Peter Piot, executive director of UNAIDS, reported that by mid-1996 more than nine million children had lost their mothers to AIDS, ninety percent of these in sub-Saharan Africa. What the statistics couldn't show were the additional millions of silent carriers who would leave children behind during the next few years.

Africa's extended family system is going through traumatic change as a result of the AIDS crisis. Normally, when children lose one or both parents, the extended family steps in to fill the gap. With so many extended family members either infected by or themselves dead from the disease, such responsibilities cannot easily be fulfilled. To add to these inordinate difficulties, the increase in orphans per family comes at a time when the traditional family is already stressed to the point of collapse under intolerable economic pressures.

Throughout AIDS-stricken Africa, the HIV virus is spread almost entirely by heterosexual intercourse, meaning that most infected individuals are women. The disease is transmitted to them by males who often have several partners. The weak position of women in relation to men in many of these countries limits their ability to insist upon use of condoms. A married woman does not dare to suggest condom use even if she knows herself to be one of several partners, or if she suspects her husband to be ill. Even prostitutes report the annoyance of customers when use of a condom is suggested. With such a high rate of infection among sexually active adults, children are at significant risk of losing one or both parents and of being infected themselves. The loss of a mother is generally more difficult than the loss of a father, because in these societies the mother is usually the one responsible for the care and well-being of the children. Thus, the loss of maternal care increases a child's vulnerability to exploitation and abuse.

Children are usually infected by their mothers during pregnancy, childbirth, or breast-feeding. It has been shown that when pregnant HIV-positive women receive intensive treatment with so-called anti-AIDS drugs such as AZT, the chances of the child's infection are greatly reduced. Birth by cesarean section, rather than allowing the child into the birth canal, is another way of reducing the infection rate in newborns. But it is the rare African woman who has the opportunity and means to undergo such treatments, and there are inhibitions to birth by cesarean section. Nevertheless, in July 1999 Uganda began testing a new drug. This drug, Nevirapine Supplement, is made of a natural substance, and has proven itself to be quite successful in preventing the passing of the virus to newborns. Its hope for Africa also lies in its cost of only $4.00 per woman for complete treatment, as compared to $1,000 for AZT.

Signs of Hope

Even in the midst of seeming disaster, there is hope. Nearly all of the affected countries have begun programs to raise awareness, with Uganda one of the first. South Africa, Zambia, Botswana, Nigeria, and others have targeted young people between fifteen and twenty-five years of age. Many NGOs have joined to assist these populations. Nevertheless, although there has been some change for the better, the rapid rate of new infection leaves much ground to be covered.

In 1986 Janet Museveni, wife of Ugandan president Yoweri Museveni, started the Ugandan Women's Effort to Save Orphans (UWESO) to save orphans created by Uganda's civil war. When the AIDS epidemic hit, UWESO shifted its focus to deal with AIDS orphans. UWESO defines an orphan as any child who has lost at least one parent. Uganda has approximately 1.5 million orphans.

Thousands of women in the rural areas are involved in the program, which focuses on community-based fostering. They assist the women by providing school fees for the orphans in primary school and later funding their vocational and artisan training.

Through UWESO, the women have the opportunity to meet other mothers who are caring for orphans, and who serve as a support group. This is very important, since these women must cope with such problems as malaria, malnutrition, health care, and shortage of medicines. UWESO, through its micro-financing scheme, also encourages women to become petty traders and participate in local markets. The women receive loans of up to $100 to set up small kiosks for the sale of such items as salt, sugar, flour, vegetable oil, matches, and produce from their farms. A community development worker trains the women in business management, banking, and credit. Through such means the women are helped to establish the psycho-social and economic base needed for the long-term well-being of the orphans.

Nevertheless, although some positive things are happening as people begin to face the enormity of the problem, taken as a whole, the AIDS crisis in sub-Saharan Africa continues to have a devastating effect on every aspect of life, and a vastly greater effort than the current one will be needed to turn it around in the years ahead.

Malnutrition

> Malnutrition is rarely regarded as an emergency; the children affected are not facing famine and betray few or no obvious signs. Yet the largely invisible crisis of malnutrition is implicated in more than half of all child deaths worldwide and violates children's rights in profound ways, compromising their physical and mental development and helping perpetuate poverty. More widespread than many suspect—with one out of every three children affected—malnutrition lowers the productivity and abilities of entire societies.
>
> ——— The State of the World's Children 1998, UNICEF

Children have the right, recognized in international law, to good nutrition. Under the Convention on the Rights of the Child, governments recognize the right of all children to the highest attainable standards of health, to facilities for the treatment of illness, and for the rehabilitation of health—specifically including the right to good nutrition and its three vital components: food, health, and care. Good nutrition is a right because it is "in the best interest of the child."[1] States are actually required under Article 24 to "take appropriate measures to reduce infant and child mortality, and to combat disease and malnutrition through the use of readily available technology and through the provision of adequate, nutritious foods and safe drinking water".[2]

What Is Malnutrition?

Malnutrition is usually the result of a combination of inadequate dietary intake, insufficient vitamin and mineral intake, and infection. A diet that does not include sufficient protein and energy-building foods, and lacks essential vitamins such as vitamin A, as well as sufficient fatty acids, will result in malnutrition.

There is no single kind of malnutrition. It can take a variety of forms appearing in combination and contributing to each other, such as protein-energy malnutrition, iodine deficiency disorders, and deficiencies of iron and vitamin A, to name just a few. However, each kind of malnutrition is the result of diverse reasons: household access to food, child and maternal care, safe water and sanitation, and access to basic health services.[3]

Social, political, economic, and cultural factors also contribute to malnutrition. In regions where the culture favors men, there is likely to be malnutrition. In most parts of Africa women are responsible for the food supply, yet their own nutritional intakes may be insufficient if they do not get enough to eat or if they are denied the right to eat certain foods that are reserved for men. A lack of education can cause malnutrition because women need to be taught how to combine and prepare locally available foods in the most nutritious way. They need to know how to provide safe water and a sanitary environment. They need to learn how to recognize illnesses such as diarrheal dehydration and anemia, and what to do about them. As expectant mothers, women need to understand how to take care of their bodies and protect their unborn children.

One of the main causes of malnutrition is poverty. Children in impoverished situations often lack nutritious diets because the necessary combinations of foods are not always available or affordable. Especially in rural areas, African families depend largely on such staples as rice, corn, millet, or yams, consuming little else. These foods, because they are heavy, serve the purpose of filling the stomach, enabling children to sleep through the night without crying for food. All feel that they have eaten.

Personal Observation

What we noticed in Zaire [now Democratic Republic of Congo] is that there is a three-month-long period of famine each year—a time when the crops of the previous harvest have been consumed but the new crop is not yet ready. It seems that this can be avoided if the planting season is altered a bit so that food will always be available. During this period the children survive on mangoes. Before daylight they are out of their homes in search of mangoes. Even adults depend on the energy derived from the sugar in the mangoes to get them through the day. Not even the elements hinder the search for mangoes as children come out naked even during terrible thunderstorms to pick up the mangoes that have fallen because of the fierce winds. Many are struck by lightning, but hunger is more powerful than the risk.

The lack of adequate food preservation methods also contributes to malnutrition. Although sun-drying and smoking techniques are in use, most foods, particularly perishables, are consumed when they are in season. So, although a region may have a sufficient variety of food crops and fruits, their seasonal nature without preservation methods limits good nutrition.

The World Food Program

The World Food Program (WFP) is the food aid organization of the United Nations. It responds to food needs associated with emergencies and development, often in conjunction with the Food and Agriculture Organization (FAO) and the International Fund for Agricultural Development (IFAD). It provides food aid for victims of natural and man-made disasters; to schools, community programs, and health clinics for distribution to those in need; and in exchange for work on development projects.

WFP recognizes the special nutritional needs of children and works hand-in-hand with UNICEF on a number of projects to attack malnutrition and fight for the elimination of hunger. In crisis situations, WFP and UNICEF have joined to provide supplementary feeding programs for young children. They combined their resources to aid in the demobilization of child soldiers in the Democratic Republic of Congo (the former Zaire), and also set up a center to feed displaced children and help them be reintegrated into their societies. They have assisted drought victims in Zambia with a high-energy protein supplement, and in Madagascar with school kits, equipment, and meals.

The eradication of malnutrition is a global goal and must be taken on as a global initiative. The work of agencies such as UNICEF and WFP must be extended by governments and civic groups. Africa continues to record the highest rate of mortality among children, 11 million dying before the age of five from diarrhea, measles, malaria, or malnutrition. The poor must be encouraged to assist their governments in the identification of priorities and in managing responsibly what might well be increasingly scarce resources.

Access to Safe Drinking Water

In developing countries, waterborne and sanitation-related diseases kill well over three million people each year and disable hundreds of millions more, most of them under five years of age. Some diseases are spread through contaminated drinking water; others through food, hand-to-mouth contact, or person-to-person contact. Some are transmitted when skin and nematode come together in unsanitary waters. Examples are schistosomiasis, causing anemia and enlargement of liver and spleen; trachoma, the leading cause of blindness in humans; and hookworm, which causes anemia, gastrointestinal disturbance, and other problems.

Of all the developing regions, sub-Saharan Africa has the lowest degree of access to safe water, and the highest mortality rate from water-related diseases. In Abidjan, Ivory Coast, for example, 38 percent of the city's population of almost three million have no access to piped water, and 15 percent have no toilets and must defecate in the open.

Personal Observation

Since 1981, when I first arrived in Nigeria, water problems have become increasingly worse as more and more areas of the country are stricken by drought and the effects of polluted water sources. The reality today is a riverine area where even whole villages suffer from river blindness and its accompanying skin diseases. In the oil-producing delta areas such as Warri, water pollution has destroyed the fishing industry and severely limited farming. With no other industry and no employment opportunities, young people in this area have become extremely belligerent toward the Shell Oil Corporation, engaging in acts of sabotage of equipment, and the kidnaping of Shell employees. Kidnaping has turned into a lucrative business for these unemployed young people who feel exploited by Shell—which has not compensated these communities in adequate fashion—since neither the rivers nor the land on which they live offers any promise for a normal life.

In the dry north, where for the past two years there has not been enough rainfall to cover riverbeds, one gets water from wherever one can. Cholera and typhoid are endemic, costing the lives of hundreds of children during each dry season. We were privileged in that we had a well and a borehole. But the very dry months of March and April, when temperatures reached upward of 100 degrees each day, were extremely trying times and tests of our faith as our well ran dry and our borehole could only be pumped once a day because the pump ran too hot. The fears and doubts associated with our humanity often brought about a sense of self-preservation rather than sharing, as the demands of the community on our shrinking water supply increased and impatience crept in, as we discovered that our gateman was charging everyone a fee per bucket of water.

Clean, Safe Water

Nearly everywhere throughout Africa there is a need for clean, safe drinking water, affecting every facet of life. Bacterial and viral diseases contracted through the drinking of contaminated water include cholera, typhoid, childhood diarrheal ailments, infectious hepatitis, and poliomyelitis. Drinking water may also be contaminated with parasites causing river blindness and guinea worm, in which ingested larvae mature internally, eventually bursting through the skin.

Although the boiling of water would help in the prevention of many illnesses, most poor people, even when they know that this is best for them, are hindered because they cannot afford the fuels and receptacles needed for the preparation of potable water. The treating of city water (when a faucet or pump is available) is often inadequate because government cutbacks also affect the availability of the necessary chemicals. More and more, even in the cities, people depend on rain water or water brought in for sale in tankers or by push cart water vendors. Frequently, even this water is drawn from contaminated sources without treatment, although governments do provide designated taps, wells, streams, and boreholes from which vendors may draw water for sale to the public. Many vendors refuse to use such sources because of a small surcharge, despite warnings about public safety.

Broken pipes with water gushing out onto the ground are a familiar sight. The water is collected by bucket-carrying individuals to be used for everything from food preparation to bathing to the washing of clothes. Often, women and children come to such open pipes and wash clothing and/or themselves on the spot, avoiding the need to make numerous water-carrying trips to their homes which might be some distance away and, in any case, not contain anything large enough to store a supply of water. During the dry season even reservoirs go dry, and life centers around the endless search for water. Streets and byways are crowded from early morning until late at night as women and children search for water.

Clean water is a source of life and good health (Is. 55:10). Under the Convention on the Rights of the Child, governments are bound by law to prevent outbreaks of disease and death by providing clean, safe water for their populations.

2
Children's Education: A Lack of Good Schooling

"My people are destroyed for lack of knowledge." (Hosea 4:6)

At the start of the twenty-first century, nearly one billion people are still not able to read and write. Functional illiterates, the victims of societies which did not provide them with access to basic education, or where the schools were substandard, or where schooling was denied because they were female. Unless such situations are seriously addressed and improved, the opportunities for many African young people will diminish even further, their aspirations crushed, their hopes thwarted by an inescapable cycle of poverty and ignorance.

"Education for All" is UNICEF's focus in *The State of the World's Children 1999*. No longer is the world prepared to accept illiteracy or tolerate that children continue to be denied the right to a quality education. No one can deny the role of education in bringing about positive social change. According to the report, "it is also the single most vital element in combating poverty, empowering women, safeguarding children from exploitative and hazardous labor, and sexual exploitation. It is critical in promoting human rights and democracy, protecting the environment, and controlling population growth." [4]

Once seen as a major factor for bridging the gap between Africa and the western world, as well as the only means of upward mobility for individuals, education has suffered a serious blow as school systems on the continent lag far behind the rest of the world. In 1990, literacy rates in most African countries were still under 50 percent. Few African countries have attained free primary education for all. In some, primary education is not yet mandatory. And at the secondary level, matters are even worse. The desperate economic situation throughout much of Africa has made it impossible for many parents to pay the required school fees. And it has destroyed the motivation of many young people who find that money earned in menial employment (ranging from petty trading to vice) is more rewarding than attending school.

Sadly, while Article 28 of the Convention on the Rights of the Child recognizes the right of children to an education, and while most African countries have signed the convention, its implementation, so far, has not happened.

In sub-Saharan Africa, over 40 million children of primary school age are not in school. In rural areas, enrollment is down because of desperately inadequate facilities, creating difficulties in teacher recruitment. At times, these outlying areas seem cut off even from their own boards of education.

In North Africa, four out of five children are in school. But, just as in sub-Saharan Africa, the rural areas have less enrollment than the urban areas. Both regions have suffered because of internal problems. In the north, conflicts in Algeria and Sudan have led to school closings, loss of teachers, and increased dropout rates. In the south, the problems are associated with finance, large class sizes, poor teacher education, inadequate facilities, and a lack of learning materials.

Facilities, especially in primary schools, are often in very bad condition because of constant wear without maintenance. Because some schools have no furnishings at all, students are forced to bring their own desks and chairs or simply find stones to sit on. In some school buildings broken windows have not been replaced, and weather damage, such as blown off roofs, has not been repaired. While this is not generally true, it is, nevertheless, common in heavily indebted or economically distressed states, the condition of the schools relating directly to the amount of money put into education by the government.

Not surprisingly, the level of care and maintenance depends on how people regard government property and money. In some places it is viewed as belonging to no one, and so it receives little attention. Where people realize that it belongs to all of them, the level of care and maintenance is significantly higher. However, even where education is a priority, people may not take care of the property because it belongs to a government that they feel is not working for their best interests.

At the secondary and post-secondary levels, the number of students in school decreases. In all, only four to five percent of the secondary age group are in school, and only one percent of the post-secondary group continues. Those who do go on are unlikely to specialize in science or technology because they rarely have access to equipped labs, and the textbooks are often many years old. Some teachers, rather than relying on textbooks, have begun to sell notes which they compose for their classes. It earns them extra money, and school administrators ignore the practice. It is not unusual to have computer courses with no computers or with several that must suffice for 200 students or more. Most students struggle through to get a grade and then go to a private firm for hands-on experience. Polytechnics and trade schools all lack the materials to deliver quality education. Specialized areas such as medicine and pharmacy reflect the same needs. Schools also lack such basics as water, electricity, and furnishings.

In the developed world, even primary students have access to the most advanced tools of information technology. Many use the internet as a research tool for homework assignments. Public libraries also house a wealth of information ready to be used by anyone who chooses to do so. Most African universities, polytechnics, and teachers' colleges are yet to be exposed to such technology. Nor do they have useful libraries.

While it is a given that quality education is crucial for the success of any nation, in many regions of Africa the incentives for its delivery do not exist. African teachers are very poorly paid and in some countries are owed many months of back pay. The profession was hard hit by the financial austerity of the 1980s when governments throughout the developing world cut spending in order to meet the requirements of structural adjustment. In the resulting monetary crunch, some states must decide whom to pay from month to month. Usually the military is paid first, then others in order of priority. Teachers are very low on that list. Although in private institutions the pay is still very low, it is usually as regular as the school fees out of which they are paid.

Personal Observation

In Nigeria during the 1997-1998 school year, salaries for teachers in government schools were N800 per month. A bag of rice, the staple in the region, sold for N1,200. This meant that a teacher who was the breadwinner could not afford to purchase the staple that would feed his family for the next month. In our own UMC school in Nigeria we tried to keep up with the cost of rice by paying our teachers N1,300 per month. But, alas, the cost of the rice out-distanced our budgetary capacity by rising to N2,200 per bag by May 1998.

Throughout the 1980s and 1990s, real income declined for teachers in Africa. Primary teachers receive less than half the amount of the household absolute poverty line. Many supplement their income by offering private lessons or tutorials and by running their own private businesses—sometimes on the school premises, always to the detriment of their performance and attendance in school.

The problem of unqualified teachers also continues to plague Africa's educational systems. The responsibility for this rests with those in charge of teacher training: 1. methodologies and proper disciplinary methods need to be included in the training process; 2. the idea that one needs little education to teach elementary school needs to be challenged. Clearly, when teachers cannot master the curriculum, or when their education is deficient, quality teaching will not result.

Education for Disabled Children

> **Personal Observation**
>
> On a recent visit to a school for the blind in Taraba State, Nigeria, I was made keenly aware of how a vital part of society can just be left out of the scheme of things by the government. The school consisted of one very large room. In one corner of the room were four benches. In another corner were old braille machines and papers that were so old they had turned yellow, some eaten by rats. A third corner contained dried grass and old dirty rags which were going to be made into mattresses, so they told me.
>
> The students were all sitting outside under a tree doing nothing. They expressed fatigue because they had not eaten. They were drawn from all of the thirty states and were there on state scholarships, but there was no food or lodging for them. Most slept on a straw mat which they rolled out on the floor of the schoolroom at night. There were no toilets or bathing facilities at the school. They were waiting for their director to return from a meeting with the governor in hopes that they would get some food and some supplies.

This sad but typical case is repeated throughout Africa, reflecting the general opinion that the abilities of disabled persons and their contributions to society are limited. The blind, deaf, and physically-disabled are perhaps the most educationally disadvantaged persons in Africa. According to UNESCO, in the developing world fewer than one percent of children with special needs make it into educational systems. In addition to a lack of personnel trained to handle special needs, there is a lack of the necessary facilities. In many countries help of this sort comes from international nongovernmental organizations (NGOs) and religious groups through a range of specialized individuals.

A case strikingly opposite to the one above is the Uhuru Mchanganyiko Primary School in Tanzania. It is one of the oldest in the country and one of the first to accept children with disabilities and mainstream them into classes with other students. Of Uhuru's 1,200 students, 62 are blind, 11 are deaf-blind, and 55 have mental disabilities.

The blind and visually impaired students at Uhuru are integrated into the regular student body beginning with their third year at the school. Before beginning their regular classes, they are given a total orientation of the facility and its campus, and special instruction in academic areas. Eight specialized teachers and eight blind teachers (themselves graduates of the school) work together with mainstream teachers to give students every opportunity for success. The school operates on a shoestring, although there are plans to involve parents and the community in fund-raising activities. Despite such financial limitations, the students are achieving, and the school's track record is impressive.

A visit to any of the annual conferences will confirm that much more needs to be done in the area of services for the handicapped and mentally ill. The number of young people affected grows by the day, and it seems to be the one area where the church lacks a mission. Yes, the research had been done and the possibilities discussed, but, given the enormity of the problem, we have barely begun.

Education for Girls

> Again she conceived and bore a son, and said, "Now this time my husband will be joined to me, because I have borne him three sons . . . ." (Gen. 29:34)

Estimates show that throughout Africa there is a significant gap between the number of boys and the number of girls attending school. In some regions this stems from religious practices, in others from cultures that discriminate against females, in yet others from poverty. The words from Genesis cited above express the pain and sorrow of many women in Africa today. They also clearly present the view that classifies females as second-class citizens.

Even today, sons are of special significance to African families. Because of this, a wife is under pressure from day one of the marriage to produce male children. In traditional societies, the birth of sons guaranteed the husband's affection and the woman's place in the family. This tradition disturbs the peace and tranquility even of Christian families when the male heir is slow in coming. If he fails to appear after what tradition terms a reasonable length of time, or after a succession of females, a husband may succumb to pressure and take a second wife or concubine. Many are the stories of families torn apart by this view.

Even as families abandoned other traditional practices, the preference for male children still prevailed. To this day, the reality is male-dominated societies, legal systems partial to males, and low self-esteem and lack of opportunities for females.

Personal Observation

A young couple in our church married and the next day the couple was presented to the congregation during the morning worship service. they looked so lovely and so happy, dressed in matching outfits. The groom took the microphone and in his own way expressed his love and devotion to his wife. Surprisingly, as we were leaving the church yard I saw the bride walking down the road with two of her friends, and the groom going in another direction with a group of his friends. I asked those riding with us what was happening. The response from an older woman was that the groom didn't owe the bride anything else. "He has done his part; he has married her," she said. "You will never see them together in public again." A very sad statement, but true.

If because of poverty a family has to choose whether to educate a son or a daughter, it will prefer to educate the son, believing that his education will benefit the family. The girl, they reason, will marry into another family, and the money spent on her education will have been wasted. Although sons are the traditional caretakers of their parents in a society without social security, medicare, welfare, or other social assistance, it is being recognized that daughters generally take better care of their parents, even after marriage, than do sons. Furthermore, there is a growing tendency to educate the most intelligent of the children, whether male or female.

Still, "discrimination against girls is the largest impediment to achieving 'Education for All.' According to the World Declaration of Education for All in 1990, the most urgent priority was to ensure access to and improve the quality of education for girls . . . and to remove every obstacle that hampers their active participation." [5]

The cause of education for girls has been taken up in Africa by the forum for African Women Educationalists (FAWE). This group of professional educators has formulated an agenda on behalf of African women:

- Girls and women are the intellectual resource in Africa that will contribute to the crucial change that the continent is looking for.
- Girls must not only be educated, they must also be accorded the opportunity to use their education and their skills to make decisions about and be participants in the development of Africa.

FAWE has been active since 1992, and has successfully lobbied the ministers of education in several African countries to change policies that exclude girls from school. They support grassroots efforts with grants and awards to individuals and institutions that have found cost-effective, innovative, and replicable ways of promoting girls' education and gender equality in education. The activities of FAWE in eight countries—Burkino Faso, Ethiopia, Ghana, Guinea, Kenya, Malawi, Sierra Leone, and Zambia—have received international recognition. But perhaps its greatest contribution is changing the perception of girls' education, minister by minister and country by country. [6]

The African Girls' Education Initiative now operates in more than twenty countries and is supported by UNICEF and the Canadian and Norwegian governments. Its main goal is to help countries try different approaches to closing the gender gap in education, with the hope of improving educational systems overall. The organization believes that the benefits to African societies of educating girls are as follows:

- The more educated the mother is, the more infant and child mortality is reduced.

- Children of more-educated mothers tend to be better nourished and suffer less from illness.
- Children (particularly daughters) of more-educated mothers are likely to be educated themselves and become literate.
- The more years of education women have, the later they tend to marry and the fewer children they tend to have.
- Educated women are less likely to die in childbirth.
- The more educated a woman is, the more likely she is to have opportunities and life choices, and avoid being oppressed and exploited by her family or social situation.
- Educated women are more likely to be receptive to, participate in, and influence development initiatives and send their own daughters to school.
- Educated women are more likely to play a role in political and economic decision-making at community, regional, and national levels. [7]

What of the Future?

Parents lament the deplorable state of education in Africa, and many pray for a return to the days when those old standards will be revived. It has been argued, however, that, along with redefining the purpose of their efforts in education, African educators need to devise locally appropriate courses rather than copying the educational systems of the ex-colonial powers. Nevertheless, under those systems parents could be sure that, at worst, the child would be able to read, write, and master the language of instruction. In some states today that is the best a parent can hope for from public education. Nearly all who can afford to do so, have private teachers for their children to make up for what they do not get in the public schools. This is the only way to ensure that the child will pass state and regional exams.

Continuing the colonial systems of education, though narrow in focus, was an effort to maintain the standards that many leaders of newly independent states felt had made possible their own educational success. In short, African children would still be able to benefit from western education, which, it was believed, would make them competitive with other nations of the world, and, at home, of raising their communities to western levels of prosperity. If Africa is truly to be a part of the global economy, and if the concept of the global village is to prevail, this ideal must not be abandoned. While the education system supported by the government has failed, there are others such as those of The United Methodist Church, other religious denominations, NGOs, European governments, the American government, and others, to which African children have access and which have not failed them. Some of these schools will cater only to those who can afford the fees, but UMC schools are there for all students, particularly those who are poor. Many donor churches prefer not to support educational programs, but unless you, we, all of us, help these children, they will fall so far behind the rest of the world that it will be shameful.

3
Armed Conflict and the Destruction of Childhood

What are the eyes of a child soldier supposed to look like? Felfiel Manhina's are downcast and blank in a face that rarely smiles. He is now 22, still undersized and boyish, but he was just 13 when rebel RENAMO soldiers crept into the hamlet of Taninga before dawn in 1988 to steal food and took him too. They threatened to execute him, armed him with an AK 47 assault rifle and turned him into a pitiless killing machine aimed at his family, friends and neighbors on the government side of Mozambique's civil war. "They told me I must fight in order to eat," he stutters, loath to recall those years. "I killed people. I saw their faces when I hurt them." He cannot look a questioner in the eyes. "Now," says this boy-man who lives by cutting bamboo, "life is good, because I don't have the heavy heart of a fighter."

———— "Africa Rising," Johanna McGeary and Marguerite Michaels
Time, March 30, 1998, pp. 36, 37.

Child Soldiers

The use of children in combat is a global problem. It is far more serious than one might imagine based on the scant attention it has received, according to Mike Wessels, a professor of psychology who has done extensive work in the area of conflict resolution and healing the wounds of war, particularly in Angola and Sierra Leone. "It's sobering to think that under certain conditions, practically any child could be changed into a killer, and even more sobering to see once again how easily children who have been denied an education and trained for fighting are manipulated by local political leaders," he says. "They are pawns in local conflicts because they provide a ready group for recruitment by warlords, profiteers, and groups that foment political instability." [8]

Preying on the needs of the poor in order somehow to vindicate their social failures, agitators can easily motive people for combat, especially the young. The boys who took power in Sierra Leone had in three months confiscated all the official Mercedeses, Volvos, and BMWs, and willfully wrecked them on the road. One of the coup's leaders, Solomon Anthony Joseph Musa, shot the people who had paid for his schooling" in order to erase the humiliation and mitigate the power his middle-class sponsors held over him." [9]

The Lord's Resistance Army

Of all the paramilitary bands in Africa, the Lord's Resistance Army, in Uganda, is perhaps the most sadistic. It combines witchcraft, drugs, torture, and terror tactics as tools for complete submission. Wearing flowing white robes, its leader, Joseph Kony, claims that the group is a Christian organization and that God speaks to him. He intends to take over the country and rule it according to his interpretation of the Ten Commandments. The Lord's Resistance Army has abducted nearly 10,000 teenagers who are forced to serve as laborers and soldiers.

Based in Sudan, the group employs hit-and-run tactics against Uganda, usually coming out of the jungle at night to raid and pillage. The army burns everything in its path, allowing no one to escape. Abductees are carried back across the border into base camps in Sudan. There the dehumanizing process begins by forcing the newly captured young people to kill one of their peers.

Members of the group cover their bodies with magic potions and charms which they say give them supernatural powers such as invisibility, superhuman strength, and immunity to bullets. The mixture of witchcraft, drugs, terror, and torture causes such a degree of mental distortion that those who escape find it nearly impossible to resume a normal life. Ironically, if escapees are caught by the Sudanese, they are returned to the LRA where they are tortured and killed as an example to others.

The Ugandan government has declared all-out war on the LRA, and vowed to eliminate it. Unfortunately, they have had little success because the LRA goes underground when the heat is on, surfacing in remote areas if the need arises.

—— "A Teenage Nightmare," Merri Rosenberg, *Scholastic Update*, December 8, 1997, pp. 4-6.

Why are the numbers of child soldiers increasing? While forced recruitment accounts for the largest percentage, others join government or rebel forces voluntarily. Desperation, poverty, fear, hunger, and the need for protection are only some of the reasons why children become volunteers. A few report that they joined in the hope of avenging the death of parents and loved ones. Others have come to respect the power and fear that is generated by possession of a gun.

Initially the children may be engaged in such tasks as fetching water or wood, or as bodyguards, sentries, and spies. Girls usually cook or tend to the wounded, although they are also forced to provide sexual services or be "married off" to other soldiers. Ultimately, both boys and girls face combat, even committing atrocities against their own families as a means of showing allegiance to the group and the lack of respect for human life they must develop in order to survive.

The Machel Report

One of the most detailed and comprehensive reports on the plight of children in armed conflict was written for the United Nations by Mrs. Graça Machel, former first lady and minister of education in Mozambique (now the wife of Nelson Mandela). Serving as an expert appointed by UN General Secretary Boutros Boutros-Ghali in 1994, Mrs. Machel led a two-year global research project, with findings that are revealing and current even today. "Millions of children are caught up in conflicts in which they are not merely bystanders, but targets." [10]

Children as deliberate targets? According to Mrs. Machel, thousands of children, mostly young boys, many under ten years of age, are forcibly recruited or seized from homes, school dormitories, and orphanages to serve in government or rebel armies. This marks the beginning of a process that will change children into killers.

Once abducted, the children are subjected to a number of brain-washing techniques, including fear, brutality, and psychological manipulation. They are often beaten, sexually exploited, given drugs to hype them up and alter their consciences, and forced to commit atrocities. With their spirits broken and their wills overcome by fear, the children become docile—willing to do whatever they are told, no matter how dangerous or horrifying. Children serve as executioners, in suicide missions, and take part in cannibalistic acts.

The forced abductions seem to have a two-fold purpose: to increase the ranks of the armies and to intimidate local communities. For example, as the abductions are carried out it is common practice for groups to rape and pillage in the villages. Machel's case study of Uganda revealed that people who resisted attacks by the Lord's Resistance Army would be cut with *pangas* [machetes]. Quite a number of victims had their lips and ears cut off in macabre rituals.

Gender-based Violence

"Rape, sexual humiliation, prostitution, and other forms of gender-based violence are heightened risks for women and girls," cites the Machel Report. The very young are considered less likely to have HIV/AIDS or other sexually transmitted diseases, increasing the vulnerability of girls ten years old or younger. However, as the report points out, young boys are also raped and forced into prostitution. The sexual exploitation of young males is increasing all over Africa, even where there is no war, because of the currently raging occult belief that a man will become rich if he has sex with another man.

The following story was told to one of Mrs. Machel's advisors by a nine-year-old Liberian girl. Such stories are common—indicative of the moral decay and insanity that prevail under conflict situations:

> I saw 10 to 20 people shot, mostly old people who couldn't walk fast. They shot my uncle
> in the head and killed him. They made my father take his brains out and throw them into

some water nearby. Then they made my father undress and have an affair with a decaying
body. Then they raped my nine-year-old cousin.

Deeply disturbing are accounts of children in flight or displaced by war. By the end of 1994, Rwanda had more than 100,000 displaced children, and by 1995, UNICEF reported that fully twenty percent of Angola's children were separated from their parents. In Zaire [now the Democratic Republic of Congo] the United Methodist Church in Zaire Central was feeding thousands of children each day until the international NGOs stepped in. Globally the numbers are in the millions, according to the estimates of Mrs. Machel. These unaccompanied children will very likely be killed, tortured, raped, or recruited as child soldiers.

Clearly, child soldiers don't just happen. They reflect the deeply flawed decision-making of adults. The crudeness and cruelty of recent conflict situations in Africa has produced an environment in which exposure to violence and training for fighting takes priority over educational opportunities and basic human rights for children. "A society that mobilizes and trains its young for war weaves violence into the fabric of life, increasing the likelihood that violence and war will be its future."[11]

The Convention on the Rights of the Child, which, as noted earlier, has been ratified by nearly all African countries, prohibits the use of children below the age of fifteen as soldiers. Several of these nations have written the CRC's general principles into their constitutions, while others have established civil codes reflecting the rights of children. Nevertheless, when it comes to internal conflicts, children continue to be drafted. As has been established in the case of abusive behavior, those who have been victims are more likely than others to become perpetrators. So, also, with those who live with violence. Those who constantly witness such violence, though not victims themselves, share the same sense of victimization.

Armed Conflict

Those conflicts and disputes among you, where do they come from? Do they not come
from your cravings that are at war within you? You want something and do not have it; so
you commit murder. And you covet something and cannot obtain it; so you engage in disputes and conflicts. (James 4: 1, 2)

For many populations in Africa, days, months, even years have been consumed by terror, deprivation, and persistent gunfire. Life has been completely altered as times that were once spent earning a living, educating the young, enjoying friends and family, have given way to bitter and often senseless conflicts. Crime and violence, particularly against individuals, has reached a critical point, causing hundreds and thousands of deaths each year. Fear and misery prevail in the land.

Each of the conflicts in Africa can be traced to selfish ambition, greed, and the desire for glory, power, and money. The national interest has lost its place on agendas charged with methods of self-deification and the establishing of personality cults.

The invasion of Liberia on Christmas Eve 1989 by Charles Taylor and 150 amateur soldiers marked a horrendous shift in the tactics and consequences of wars in Africa. "Taylor had unleashed the most deadly combat system of the current epoch: the adolescent human male equipped with a Kalashinikov—an AK 47 assault rifle."[12]

Since then, young children have increasingly become the victims of such conflicts, with boy soldiers a phenomenon that Africa and the world will not soon forget. Why the children? Countless times, those who engage children in warfare respond that it is because children are less willful, less experienced in the ways of the world, and therefore easier to control physically and psychologically. When these children kill one another, it desensitizes them to the fact of death and the act of killing, and transforms them from children into tools.[13]

In recent years there has been a marked change in the nature of armed conflict. Modern wars are seldom fought on battlefields; are increasingly ethno-political; involve attacks on civilians by paramilitary and militia groups; are low-intensity and internal; and are characterized by butchery, rape, and other violence against women and children.[14] In an article entitled "The Kalashinikov Age," Michael Klare writes about what he calls a pathology of contemporary conflict:

1. In almost every case, ethnic prejudices have been aroused by unscrupulous and ambitious demagogues in search of power and wealth.
2. Activities are carried out by militias and paramilitary bands involving attacks on civilian targets—usually of a different ethnic group.
3. Young children play a major role in the fighting, carrying out even the most extreme atrocities.
4. Ethnic hostility, poverty, and a craving for goods, rather than political, ideological or religious sentiment, usually spark these conflicts.
5. Violent attacks on women and children are common.[15]

According to Klare, the purpose of such violence is to get whatever possible from local populations in order to acquire more arms and ammunition; to get fresh recruits, often young boys for combat and young girls for sex; and to destroy people's faith in the ability of established government to protect them, which may involve driving people from their homelands.

Klare's conclusions, however, center around the availability of weapons, rather than on the underlying causes of war. While he sees poverty, corruption, and demagoguery as prime causes of conflicts, he feels that the only way to bring such conflicts to an end is to cut off the supply of arms. "Conflicts last only so long as belligerents receive a steady stream of arms and ammunition. By shutting off that stream, it should be possible to reduce both the duration and the severity of combat," writes Klare.

The supply of weapons into Africa has not received adequate attention. Trade in arms is a highly competitive and hugely lucrative business. As flare-ups continue, logic dictates that those who are able to provide arms or security gain increasing power and wealth. Power means having access to the natural wealth that can be used to purchase more arms. In the case of Sierra Leone, a geological survey of the eastern region where the rebel strongholds are will reveal some of the finest diamonds in the world, as well as gold, titanium, and bauxite. There was substantial evidence that rebel leader Johnny Paul Koroma's men were digging up diamonds and selling them abroad in order to buy weapons before they were ousted in a counter-coup in February 1998.

The same is true of Jonas Savimbi and his UNITA movement in Angola. At one time UNITA was accused of flooding the diamond market to such an extent that DeBeers, the South African diamond exporter, was threatened as the price of diamonds dropped worldwide.

Guns are cheap—often bartered for stocks of coffee, tea, minerals, or gold, in lieu of cash. Deals are also made to accept toxic waste or engage in the drug trade; to smuggle fuel or other goods in exchange for weapons.

> After four years of the uncontrolled flow of small arms into Rwanda, Burundi, Uganda, the Democratic Republic of Congo, and Tanzania, more than 1.5 million people have been killed, and another 6 million have fled their homes. More than a hundred people continue to be killed each week in military or ethnic cleansing operations. As always, bearing the brunt of army mutinies, ethnic slaughter, and civil war, are the women and children.[16]

A Vicious Circle

While there are some agreed-upon global norms against weapons of mass destruction, no such norms or standards exist to bring about a reduction in the excessive and destabilizing accumulation of small arms and light weapons. These are the weapons increasingly used as primary instruments of violence in the internal conflicts dealt with by the United Nations; they are responsible for large numbers of deaths and displacement of citizens around the world, and they consume large quantities of the UN's resources.

The excessive and destabilizing accumulation and transfer of small arms and light weapons is closely related to the increased incidence of internal conflicts and high levels of crime and violence. It is, therefore, an issue of legitimate concern for the international community. Groups and individuals operating outside the reach of state and government forces make extensive use of such weapons in internal conflicts. Insurgent forces, irregular troops, criminal gangs, and terrorist groups are using all types of small arms and light weapons . . . .

> Accumulations of small arms and light weapons by themselves do not cause the conflicts in which they are used. The availability of these weapons, however, contributes toward exacerbating conflicts by increasing the lethality and duration of violence, by encouraging a violent rather than a peaceful resolution of differences, and by generating a vicious circle of a greater sense of insecurity, which in turn leads to a greater demand for, and use of, such weapons.
>
> —— The United Nations, "General and Complete Disarmament: Small Arms,"
> UN document A/52/298, August 27, 1997, pp. 9, 10.

The Aftermath of Armed Conflict
Land Mines

When the wars are over, the victims are the human evidence that the terror continues. Nowhere is this a more profound reality than with land mines. The Machel Report candidly affirms that "few weapons of war are more lethal to children."

The land mine is a small metallic or nonmetallic device that requires very little pressure to detonate. There are two kinds: blast mines and fragmentation mines. Blast mines cripple or kill through the upward force of the explosion. Fragmentation mines spew pieces of hot steel that penetrate and tear. Mines are individually laid by hand, dropped mechanically, scattered from helicopters, or fired in bunches from artillery and rockets.

The particular danger, in addition to the damage of explosion, is that land mines may remain active for as long as fifty years. Mines laid today may kill or maim until well into the next century unless something is done to deactivate them. As weapons of war they are chosen because they are very cheap, costing only about three dollars each to manufacture. However, it can cost up to $1,000 to remove a single mine, and an expert can spend an entire day clearing just a few yards of mine-activated land.

In Africa the mines have been randomly placed, often around schools, water sources, individual homes, and agricultural land, as well as along roads, border points, and near military bases—each side in a given conflict trying to do as much damage as possible by interfering with supply lines and humanitarian aid missions.

The impact of land mines has been a total disruption of ordinary life. Agriculture has suffered, since even in areas that are being de-mined, progress is very slow. This has led to malnutrition, famine, and even starvation. Since grazing lands are affected, animal husbandry can only proceed on a limited basis. Changes in the grazing cycle have caused heavy losses of livestock. Refugees have been prevented from resettlement, and the delivery of relief materials to the needy has been hampered, air lifts becoming an expensive burden to the UN and other aid agencies. In some countries, the heavy mining of roads creates such isolation for certain villages that even medical help cannot reach them. Children injured by land mines seldom receive the care they need, and under these circumstances may receive no care at all.

Children are more likely to be victims than adults. If children cannot read the signs posted to warn them of the presence of land mines, they enter into mined areas unaware of the danger. Because their bodies are small, children are more likely to die from mine injuries. Of those survivors who are maimed, few receive prostheses that can adapt to the continued growth of their limbs. A child's bones grow faster than the surrounding tissue, therefore a wound may require repeated amputations and a new artificial limb as often as every six months. Under current circumstances in Africa, it is most unlikely that such prostheses and such continued care will be available.

Children's daily activities such as collecting firewood, fetching water, grazing animals, even engaging in outdoor play, become high-risk and potentially fatal in areas littered with landmines. Rae McGrath, director of a nongovernmental organization, the Mines Advisory Group, tells of an incident which, while not in Africa, could have happened in any landmine-infested rural situation:

> I was examining the site of a mine incident . . . where a six-year-old boy had died. The boy had strayed into a minefield while playing, but it was not clear at all how he could possibly have stood on a mine accidentally; the mines, all surface-laid pressure devices, were clearly visible, and it was unlikely that the boy, from a village in a heavily-mined area, would not have recognized them as mines. The area was grassland meadow, and it was only when I crouched to inspect the accident site that I suddenly realized why the boy had died. Although the grass was no more than six inches high, from my new position I could see no mines. I could only see grass. My eye level was roughly that of a boy of six. The victim died because he was too small.

———"Landmines: Fallout of War," Church World Service and Witness, reprinted in *New World Outlook*, Jan/Feb 1997.

Angola is said to be the most heavily mined country in Africa—and in the world, along with Cambodia—and to have the world's highest number of amputees per inhabitant: 70,000, of whom 8,000 are children. There are currently some land mine removal and victim assistance programs in place, and it is assumed that with the passage of recent legislation, as well as global awareness campaigns, efforts will multiply and offer new hope for the victims as well as for those living in heavily mined areas.

Restoration after War

Some of the greatest atrocities of the wars in Africa may have been committed when the rebel factions fled Sierra Leone in July 1999. Hundreds of people, young and old, including small babies, had their limbs systematically and deliberately cut off. At times, whole villages were victims of this scourge. In a news conference, the president of Sierra Leone held up a four-year-old child without hands and asked, "What crime has she committed?" That child is only one of many of whom the same question must be asked. How do we restore such individuals to health and hope? For many, restoration will never become a reality because the nature and scope of the problem require enormous amounts of money, medical care, and long-term attention.

Restoration for child soldiers is another area in which the effects of war are felt long after the peace has been signed. These children reportedly suffer from heightened aggression, nightmares, flashbacks, and other mental anomalies. Often addiction to drugs must be overcome and long-term psychological care provided. Grafton Camp in Sierra Leone, operated by UNICEF and local partners, was one such facility for recently demobilized child soldiers. The state of this program is not known at the time of this writing, because of the recent resumption of fighting in that country.

In Angola, a process called "traditional healing" is used to help child soldiers reintegrate into their home communities. Though it is often considered witchcraft by outsiders, its rate of success has been extraordinary. This same process has also been used in Mozambique. There it is called a psychological purgative, and offers the opportunity for atonement and relief from the spirits of those whom they have killed. If child soldiers are allowed to re-enter the society without such cleansing or healing, it is believed that they may put the entire community at risk.[17]

For young girls, especially those who have been sexually exploited, the physical and emotional scars can be compounded by negative societal attitudes. Furthermore, the abuse of their bodies may have caused various reproductive and other ailments. Some have families who are willing to take them back and support them throughout the course of the transition. Many others, however, find their communities destroyed or their families unwilling to accept them. No longer seeing themselves as children, in spite of their youth, and with little else to look forward to, some turn to prostitution, that is, commercial sexual exploitation, as a permanent means of survival.

In the aftermath of turmoil, as people try to rebuild their lives and their societies, other problems come to the fore: hunger—it may be difficult to meet nutritional needs; illness—there may be no health services or preventive drugs; water resources may be contaminated; sanitation may be lacking. Add to this recurring outbreaks of malaria, cholera, measles, and other diseases, and there may ultimately be more deaths than those caused by the fighting.

4
The Shattered Lives of Forgotten Children

Children in Kenya have expressed a wish to be accorded love, care, and protection. They also want the enactment of the Children's Bill (1995) hastened. This was the children's "Message for 1998" read by 12-year-old Rose Wanjugu, a standard seven pupil at Moi Nyeri Complex, during the launch of the Day of the African Child at the Catholic Diocese secretariat on Tuesday. Miss Wanjugu read the message on behalf of Kenya's 16 million children. The ceremony was marked with pomp. Many school children attended. Notably absent were the street children whose plight featured prominently at the fete. The themes covered by various performing groups were on the drug menace, child molestation, the plight of girls, AIDS, early marriage, and street children. Children from King'ong'o Primary school recited a choral verse questioning their parents' integrity in relegating their parental roles to teachers. A UNICEF officer, Mr. Greg Owino, said that the number of Kenyan children orphaned by AIDS was expected to reach 600,000 by the year 2000. The annual children's day was first commemorated on June 16, 1991, in Kenya. It is in honor of school children massacred in Soweto, South Africa, in June 1976.

———*The Nation,* Nairobi, Kenya, June 11, 1998

A pupil of Kyaggwe Road Primary School, Shatra Nabunya, has blamed elders, especially politicians, for causing wars which leave many Ugandan children dead and others suffering. In a three-page speech read at the Institute of Teacher Education Kyambogo recently and addressed to parents and government officials, Nabunya, 8 years old, blamed the current suffering and misery of children on greedy and selfish politicians. Nabunya was addressing an assembly organized by The Child-to-Child Program to celebrate The Day of the African Child. She said that during war, children are the most affected because they are left orphaned, homeless, helpless and in untold suffering. It is common to hear of children being kidnapped, defiled, tortured, enslaved and exploited. "Remember," she warned, "we are the pillars of tomorrow." She went on to explain that the young generation is worried that if the elders don't help them to survive, there will be no one to replace the elders. "I wish to bring it to your notice that we can implement our rights but elders and politicians are a roadblock in our struggle; they deny us the chance. Yet we advocate for peace, security, and freedom. . . ."

———*The Monitor,* Kampala, Uganda, July 16, 1998

Child Labor

In 1997, in its annual report *State of the World's Children,* UNICEF focused on child labor, with the aim of seeking to end hazardous and exploitative child labor. The problem is complex in Africa, where there are cultural and societal norms associated with children and work. "No doubt some of the work promotes or enhances their development without interfering with schooling, recreation and rest, however much of it is palpably destructive, with poor children facing such hazards because they are exploited," says the report.

As noted earlier, child labor, according to the Convention on the Rights of the Child, is work that uses children under fifteen years of age, as specified by the International Labor Organization (ILO). Labor is exploitative when

- children are engaged in full-time work at too early an age
- it requires many hours of work
- the work exerts undue physical, social, or psychological stress
- children are required to work and live on the streets
- pay is inadequate
- there is too much responsibility
- it hampers access to education
- it undermines children's dignity and self-esteem, such as bonded labor and sexual exploitation
- it can cause physical injury and death
- it is detrimental to full social and psychological development

There are many reasons why children in Africa work, but most do so because they have no other choice. Inflationary pressures, structural adjustment programs, unemployment, and the lifting of government subsidies on essential commodities, as well as irregular salary payments, have combined to reduce many African societies to two groups: the haves and the have-nots. Increasingly, professionals such as teachers, university professors, middle management personnel, and large numbers of health care workers are joining the ranks of the "have-nots." When families are faced with a reduction or loss of income, everyone who can make some kind of contribution is put to work, even the children.

It is by no means the desire of the parents to put their children to work. Each family would prefer to have its children in school or otherwise constructively engaged. However, when incomes barely meet what is needed for food and shelter, educational fees have no priority. In UMC schools in Africa, when parents can no longer pay school fees they continue to send the children to school until the administration is forced to send the children away. Even then parents keep the children home only until the pressure to pay the fees has subsided—and the children return, without fees.

The loss of income in a system without welfare or other social supports insures certain poverty. Thus poverty, without government incentives or assistance programs, is a major force driving children to work. "Where society is characterized by poverty and inequity, the incidence of child labor is likely to increase, as does the risk that it is exploitative." Distressingly, even though the risk is high, some families need that small income so desperately that parents refuse to acknowledge the risk.[18]

It is not uncommon in Africa to see small children hawking goods on the road, or going from door to door with small quantities of something for sale. It may be boiled eggs, bananas, peanuts, or other foods. Some of these children are barely seven years old and many are girls. They are frequently beaten by older thugs who take away their money and goods. At other times the children are sexually molested. Often, mission personnel helped make up the losses of such children when they were afraid to go home and report what had happened.

Children are also exploited by tradition. For example, in northern Nigeria's Hausa-Fulani areas tradition dictates that girls marry at a very young age. Some marriages are arranged at birth, others later, but by the time a girl is twelve years old she is usually married, although she may not yet be living in her husband's home. These young girls are required by tradition to carry certain items with them to their matrimonial homes, and they must earn the money to do so. They usually sell cooked food or fruit on the streets. This kind of work is accepted practice and is preferred over formal schooling other than Koranic school. Furthermore, these young girls are highly exploited because they are often openly fondled by male customers.

Asabe Mohammed, a fourteen-year-old food hawker from the village of Soro in Nigeria, had been on the street selling food cooked by her mother throughout her primary school years. "I think I was not that big when I started hawking food," she commented, pointing to a seven-year-old girl. But Asabe had a second chance, attending the Soro Girl-Child Education Center, established in May 1993 as part of an initiative by UNICEF and the Nigerian government [19]

Perhaps the most widespread area of child exploitation is domestic work. Since it takes place behind closed doors, and each household is unique, it is difficult to gauge its extent. However, "nine out of every ten of them are girls who are trapped in a cycle of dreary tasks amounting often to virtual slavery."[20]

A "houseboy" or "housegirl" is often considered a nonperson—part of the household for no reason but to work and follow a barrage of orders. These children are not expected to have a mind or opinion of their own. They are treated with the utmost disrespect, often called derogatory names, and physically abused by both children and adults in the home. Many orphans end up as houseboys or housegirls to family members, and even in such cases they are frequently subject to abuse.

These children work long hours, sometimes twelve to fifteen hours a day, and may be called upon at any time, day or night. "The children are often expected to sleep where they can, on the kitchen floor or in a corner of a child's room. They may live for days on bread and tea. They are paid very little, with girls earning consistently less than boys, or sometimes receiving left-over food or discarded clothing as remuneration."[21]

It is common for the anger of employers to be taken out on children who work as houseboys or housegirls. Many suffer burns and cuts—even broken bones. Unless severely injured, they rarely get professional medical help, and few attend school.

Sexual abuse is regarded by some employers as part of the terms of employment. Older girls often report being raped by males in the household, even impregnated by them. Commercial sexual exploitation or child prostitution can also present a high risk for these children. Frequently they are exposed to serious health problems, including respiratory diseases, HIV and other sexually transmitted diseases, unwanted pregnancies and abortions, and drug addiction. "We have the same place as bums do in society. No one wants to know us or be seen with us," said a fifteen-year-old Senegalese girl exploited through prostitution.[22]

A new dimension has been added by the problem of housegirls and houseboys. It has now become a sought-after form of relief for parents who can no longer afford to feed their children. Its exploitative nature is played down—often diminished to the point that local TV dramas and comedies portray the houseboy or housegirl as lazy, lying manipulators who victimize each household they enter. Furthermore, having houseboys or housegirls has become a status symbol: the more a household has, the more important its position in the eyes of the community.

There are, however, several programs that address the problems of child domestic workers. In Kenya, for example, with an estimated 200,000 of these children, the Sinaga Women and Children Child Resource Center in Nairobi provides classes in basic education and skills training.

The number of young people—generally older teenagers and young adults—hawking items in the streets is also rising, especially in Nigeria. At first only males were involved, but now there is an almost equal number of females. They sell imported goods: towels, electronics, hardware, and educational supplies, as well as bottled and bagged drinking water and fruit drinks. The young people congregate in areas with huge traffic jams or where the traffic lights last a long time. They weave in and out between cars, haggling on prices for their merchandise.

When the light changes, they run beside the moving vehicle, still hoping to close the sale or retrieve their merchandise if someone in the car has taken it for closer examination. Sometimes, paying customers simply toss the money out of the window as they take off. The young salespersons are then exposed to oncoming traffic in order to pick up the money. Sometimes they hang on to car or bus windows trying to make change while the vehicle is in full motion. For all of these reasons, many children in this trade are killed or seriously maimed.

In Nigeria such trade is unique in that it represents a boycott by one specific tribal group against an educational system that has totally failed the nation's children. Usually, though in these days not exclusively, youngsters of the Ibo tribe engage in this trade. They actually work for someone with the means to import huge quantities of goods—requiring large amounts of foreign exchange—who hires these young people as salespersons. Working on commission, they often earn as much as a mid-level civil servant. Parents are satisfied, since this has become meaningful work paying good wages. Recently other items, even those made in the home, began to be peddled in similar fashion. In an open letter, the Emir of Ilorin in Kwara State pleaded with Ibo parents to send their children back to school and put an end to this trade.

Chima Ezonyejiaku is one of these boys. His father is a retired head teacher and his mother still teaches in a village school, yet Chima has abandoned his studies to apprentice himself to a wealthy trader in the town of Onitsha. Like most of his friends, he feels that school is a waste of time, and wants to begin the process of making money. [23]

In Nigeria there are thousands of boys like Chima. Because it is unlikely that they will return to school, it will be necessary to develop educational opportunities just for them. In 1994, in the states of Abia, Anambra, Enugu, and Imo, 51 percent of boys were not in school; in 1996, it was 58 percent. UNICEF and Forward Africa, a local NGO, are helping the Nigerian government provide educational opportunities in local market places, mechanics' workshops, and Koranic schools. Classes and school hours are flexible, and the instructors emphasize reading, writing, and survival skills for present-day life.

There are also child laborers in agriculture who risk exposure to a variety of biological and chemical agents and pesticides; in mining, where they work without adequate protective equipment, training, or clothing; and in match factories, where they risk fire and explosions.[24]

A concerted attack on Africa's deeply rooted poverty would greatly reduce the number of children vulnerable to exploitation at work. This could easily be tackled by governments in the following ways: 1. by admitting that what they [the governments] are presently doing is not working and that, even if it were, it is insufficient; and 2. by setting relevant educational goals based on the reality of their environments.

Street Children

Various political and socioeconomic factors account for the tremendous increase in the number of children and adults who live on the streets of Africa's cities. With few skills and no resources, the homeless are on the streets trying to eke out some kind of life for themselves. They may be orphans or refugees displaced by war or famine, or former rural dwellers who, unable to grab a foothold in the city, have fallen victim to poverty and the dynamics of the street.

Much of Jesus' ministry was directed toward disadvantaged people just like these. And as Christians we, too, are directed to show love and compassion for those in need. We may be able to do little about the circumstances that put them into such difficulties, but we are in duty bound to try.

> For I was hungry and you gave me food, I was thirsty and you gave me something to drink, I was a stranger and you welcomed me, I was naked and you gave me clothing, I was sick and you took care of me, I was in prison and you visited me. . . . just as you did it to one of the least of these who are members of my family, you did it to me.(Matt. 25:35-36, 40)

For African children, usually the end of wars means the beginning of life on the streets. Former child soldiers who have no family or community to return to; females formerly held by military groups, now turning to prostitution for survival; orphans and refugee children looking for food—all can be found on the streets in increased numbers once a regional conflict is ended. This is true even of families: those driven from rural areas because of the fighting; those who were in hiding during the conflict; those who cannot return to their land because of land mines, polluted water, and other environmental factors. All swell the number of people seeking survival on the streets.

At times, children without families form small groups that serve as loose support systems, offering some protection. Although some of these groups have been known to grow very cohesive, serving as surrogate families, generally it is every person for him- or herself.

There's a street in one of the nicer parts of Luanda where children live packed into storm drains underneath the road. People passing see young heads peering out of the gutters. They are small children who were separated from their families during the war, or whose parents are too poor to support them. They sleep in the drains because it is safer than sleeping in the streets.

―― BBC, Focus on Africa, July-September 1998, p. 51.

In South Africa, the problem of street children has risen to alarming heights. When apartheid ended, thousands of young people left the rural areas in search of jobs and other amenities denied them for so long. Disillusionment and frustration soon set in as neither the jobs nor the opportunities materialized, Some were unable to return home; most were unwilling. Most of them swapped their dreams for life on the streets. The result in most urban areas was a rise in juvenile prostitution, child alcoholism, and drug addiction.

Social service agencies were overwhelmed with the magnitude of the problem. Government officials and NGOs working with marginalized children enlisted the services of the University of South Africa in an effort to deal with the problem. The findings of a study by the departments of urban studies and sociology are discussed in the following paragraphs:

Street Children. According to police sources, approximately 10,000 to 12,000 homeless young people were concentrated in large cities throughout the country. The majority of these children—boys as well as girls—were engaged in prostitution. Their plight was blamed on the breakdown of the family under apartheid. Fathers were hardly ever at home, being forced to live in hostels and other camps related to their employment, often far away from home. Most mothers worked as domestics, living in their places of employment and returning home once a month or even less. Out of cruel necessity, many of South Africa's street children had essentially been abandoned by both parents.

Juvenile Prostitution. Unlike other parts of the world, it was established that in South Africa juvenile prostitution has no links to organized crime. Police records revealed that in Johannesburg alone there were approximately 3,000 children between the ages of twelve and sixteen regularly engaged in prostitution. Half of them worked in the townships of Soweto, Alexandra, and Tokoza, and the rest in Hillbrow, Joubert Park, Berea, and Yeoville. The young prostitutes answered a number of questions for the survey, as follows: 1. *Why did you become a prostitute?* Because we were on the streets (80 %). [This suggested that if taken off the streets, they would no longer engage in prostitution.] 2. *Why are you on the streets?* a. Because our parents were separated (60%); b. Because our parents are dead (20%); c. Because we were fleeing a step-parent (10%); d. Because we didn't want to go to school (6%); e. Because we came to search for our parent/s in the city (2%); f. For no particular reason (2%). The work environment for young prostitutes is very difficult since there are continuing scuffles between them and adult prostitutes. The adults have marked out their own specific territory, and have vowed to defend it.

Alcoholism. Drinking has caught on with youth on the streets. Under apartheid, even adults were not allowed to be drunk on the streets of large cities. Now it is common to see children who are barely adolescents drinking strong beers in public bars. They earn the money through prostitution. Bar owners without scruples even set aside special areas in their establishments to accommodate them. The following answers were given by child alcoholics between the ages of eleven and sixteen: 1. *Under what circumstances did you take your first drink?* a. At a party or celebration with friends (38%); b. In the family circle (15%); 2. *Why do you drink?* a. To forget worries or problems (35%); b. To mimic adults (25%); c. For pleasure (25%); d. Because my friends drink/To impress my friends (10%); e. I don't know (5%).

Drugs. Only recently has South Africa declared a war on drugs. Once again, those most exposed are street children, not only as consumers but also as sellers, in order to get easy money. Twelve percent of the street children interviewed admitted to taking drugs on a regular basis; 22 percent, to having tried drugs at least once. Under apartheid there were no laws regarding black street children, since their very presence in the cities was illegal. The new South African constitution includes the rights of children and students as fundamental and guaranteed. And in 1994, the South African parliament adopted a law prohibiting violence against minors, including sexual exploitation.

In 1997 it was reported that of the 18,000 known cases of violence against children, 4,000 related to rape, 2,500 to incest, and 99 in which adults sexually exploited children. Locally a special police unit (the Child Protection Unit) was set up to address the problem. An NGO, the National Infant and Children's Rights Organization, is working in the townships surrounding Johannesburg and in some of the city's neighborhoods to stop child prostitution. They have set up a vocational center to help marginalized children learn a trade. Also, UNICEF has launched a vast national medication campaign.

[The full text of this study can be found in *Jeune Afrique Economie,* May 1998, "Quand la Jeunesse Noire S'en Joie."]

Personal Observation

We, too, can help—and for very little. One night in 1991, as we were passing through Kitambo Junction, a large bus and taxi stop near our residence in Kinshasa [in the former Zaire], our headlights fell on numerous hands and very exposed legs gesturing for vehicles to stop. I was not as surprised at the number of girls out there as I was at their ages. Most were in their early teens. I learned later that the older women had moved down the street to avoid the menace of these young girls.

Just a few months earlier, I had been working in a UMC program in the Lubumbashi area, which sought to get girls out of prostitution by teaching them sewing and tailoring, and upon graduation helping them secure a sewing machine at a reduced price in order to go into business for themselves. I decided to try the same thing in Kinshasa. With the help of the Women's Fellowship, we made contact with some of these girls and started a sewing circle under a tree in the yard of Ozone UMC with twenty-two of them, ranging in age from eleven to sixteen. With a single donation of $300, the girls were provided with cloth, scissors, a tape measure, needles, thread, and a Bible.

Many of the girls did not attend any church and did not know how to pray. Our ninety-minute sessions three times a week consisted of Bible study and hand sewing. I was assisted by two women who handled the evangelism sessions in the local language. As we wrote our newsletters home, we never failed to mention what God was doing in this group, and the donations continued to come: ten dollars here, twenty dollars there, and the continued support of Kingswood UMC in Newark, Delaware. Then, through funds made available by the area secretary, the sewing machines were bought.

Eventually, we were able to play a more positive role in the day-to-day living situations of the girls by providing medical care, food, clothing, and rent when needed. They all became members of Ozone UMC, and were recognized as the only teenage foyer in the annual conference.

<u>Slavery</u>

Slavery has a long history in Africa, and the fact that it has resurfaced, along with cannibalism, witchcraft, human sacrifice, and other practices long abandoned, is a matter for profound concern. The sale of individuals has reached alarming proportions, with official estimates suggesting that more than one million women and children are sold throughout the world each year. It has long been claimed as an issue in Mauritania and Mali, although both governments dismiss such claims as false. Recent attention has been focused on the Sudan, because of the efforts of Christian Solidarity International (CSI), a Swiss-based human-rights association that has been paying Arab traders large sums of money to recover members of the Dinka tribe who have been sold into slavery.

Slavery is big business in the interior of Sudan. As a practice it has existed for centuries, but died out by the time of independence in 1956. The outbreak of civil war in 1983 ushered in its renewal. Slavery has become a military tactic, and is encouraged by the government in Khartoum. Whole Dinka communities have been destroyed, with people, cattle, and grain plundered as booty of war. Thousands of southerners have been abducted by Arab slavers and sold into bondage with the knowledge and consent of the government.

Aside from abductions, agents canvass rural areas, particularly those in the greatest economic distress, and establish friendships with parents and children. They promise work, money, and other benefits in order to persuade parents to let the children go with them. It is said that parents are aware of what will happen to their children, but because of the extreme hardship of their lives they take the money and send their children away.

As is also the case in other parts of Africa, the Sudanese government categorically denies the existence of slavery. Instead, it says it is only the taking of hostages, which is a traditional practice during tribal clashes. On a recent news broadcast Americans could see members of the CSI in action, purchasing the freedom of several hundred Dinka slaves. Whether the government admits it or not, the practice is going on within its borders, and the children suffer greatly, victimized with beatings, torture, and other forms of abuse:

I was captured in 1986 [says Deng, a young girl]. My father was killed in the attack on our village. The man who took me away came on horseback. My hands were tied, and I was made to walk for seven days with the other children they had taken. I had to work in the kitchen of this Arab's house.... When I was 14, I was told I was going to be circumcised. I didn't want it to happen, but three women held me down, and I was cut with a knife. It was very painful. The master already had a wife but he made me become his wife as well. If I refused to sleep with him, he used to beat me with a stick. His other wife was jealous and used to fight with me.[25]

Deng and her children were recently returned to her village. Other girls taken at such a young age usually end up as child prostitutes for foreign customers. An Arab trader who does business with CSI reports that "you often find farms with 30 to 40 slaves. Mostly boys who look after cattle. You can get a boy for about $63. Girls are more expensive because when they grow up they can be married."[26]

In spite of its work, CSI comes under much scrutiny. The organization is accused of encouraging the trade by offering money to buy the Dinka back. It is also said to be inflating the price of slaves as a result of its dealings. Human rights groups have put pressure on the Sudanese government, but as of this writing the practice continues, and so does the work of Christian Solidarity International.

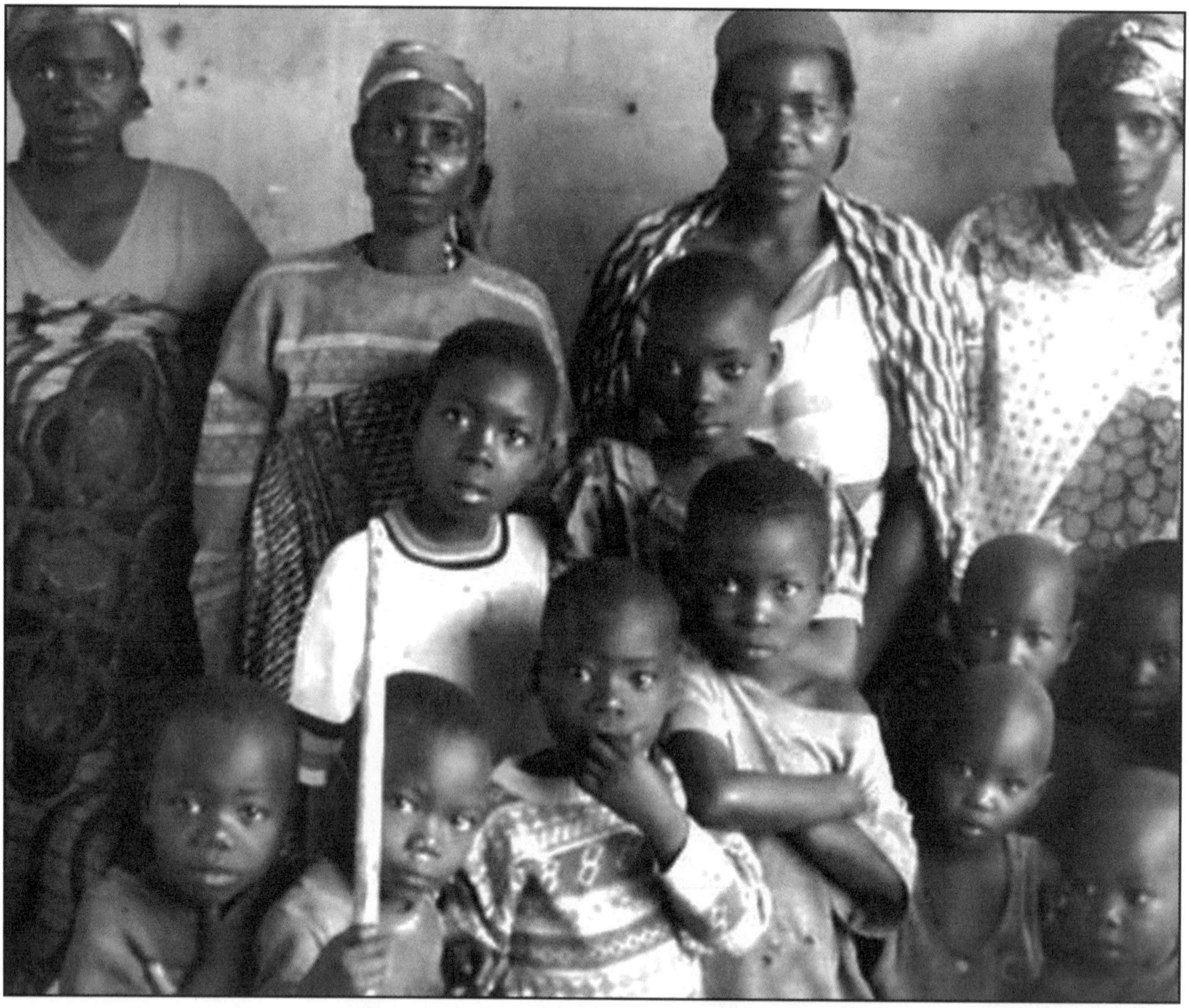

5
Decisions of Nations: Their Impact on Children

So this is Kinshasa.
What a dismal place! Everything is gray.
I see
they don't paint the cement blocks of their buildings;
they just build and leave it like that.
Ummm . . .
So many unfinished houses;
no roofs, no window panes, no doors;
only a piece of cloth, showing the wear of many hands.
Why?
Must the houses be so tiny?
Everything is done outside except sleeping.
Those little sheds behind?
Kitchen, bath, toilet.
Oh! I see . . .
Startling, glaring poverty.
I'm beginning to feel sad about it.
How can I?
Look at the children . . .
some in rags, some no clothes.
They smile, but they must be hungry.
I feel it!
God, are you sure this is where you want me to be?
I know it!

—— Onwu, *The Diary of a Missionary*, an unpublished work

As in all societies, the immediate environment plays a major role in the lives of African children. Largely a combination of economic policy, the political climate, and cultural factors, the social milieu represents all that is reality to the African child. Some understanding and awareness of the prevailing situation is crucial in efforts to formulate effective programs of high quality, as well as opportunities for mission.

Urbanization

We begin with the cities because of their tremendous recent growth. Most have expanded far beyond their original or colonial borders, often with shanty towns or makeshift ghettos on their fringes where the less fortunate make their homes. Among the contributing factors to this growth is an attraction for city life by rural dwellers who have become frustrated with the lack of opportunity and basic infrastructure in the villages. Young people from the countryside, lured by freedom from traditional bonds and ways of life, searching for work, educational opportunities and/or easy money, rush to the cities. Agricultural workers who can no longer sustain their families because of depleted soil, floods, or drought, leave the rural areas for the cities. Also forced toward the cities are refugees and those displaced by civil unrest, wars, and/or land mines. Unfortunately, like the lost son in Luke 15:1-32, and other examples, most fail to find easement, facing only a different kind of poverty.

The resulting overpopulation puts a tremendous strain on existing urban infrastructure, since in most African states little has been done toward modernization or expansion since independence. With national officials focused on the political and economic rather than the social and environmental aspects of statehood, the infrastructure of most cities has gone from neglected to deplorable in record time.

"Citizens have a right to an environment that is not harmful to their health or well-being," wrote a group of 20 students from Sinton High School in West Cape, South Africa. They saw as problems in their environment "overcrowding, unemployment, homelessness, congestion and pollution." They were most distressed by the "squatter camps which covered large areas, the growing rate of drug addiction among their [sic] peers, depression and disease." They gave as examples the fact that in Central Africa, one in five people suffers from tuberculosis; that poor sanitation and a lack of facilities has led to rampant diarrhea; and that natural vegetation is nonexistent in most areas. they called for "better public transportation, urban growth planning, government control of sanitation, air, and water quality." [27]

The United Nations, in a broad effort to promote social, economic, and cultural rights in conjunction with civil and political rights, defined the scope of what constitutes "human rights." Often considered as "needs" basic to humanity and having a direct impact on the survival of children, the UN went a step farther and elevated these "needs" to "rights." As "rights," the implication of these tenets changed, and they could no longer be passed over as cultural or religious matters or out of the realm of government. They were legal and binding and not to be ignored.

The Convention on the Rights of the Child

The idea that children have special needs has given way to the conviction that children have rights, the same full spectrum of rights as adults: civil and political, social, cultural, and economic.[28]

On September 2, 1990, after its adoption by the United Nations General Assembly, this conviction was entered into international law as the Convention on the Rights of the Child (CRC). At the time of this writing it has been ratified by almost every country on the African continent.

The idea is not new. Is this not what Jesus meant in Matthew 18:2-6? Parents and all categories of caregiver, including governments, are responsible for the proper instruction of children in the ways of God and the ways of life (Deut. 6: 1-9; Luke 1: 17), for the provision of their basic needs, and for protection from negative elements in their society and environment. The ultimate condemnation is promised for those who put children at risk by creating harmful situations (Eph. 6:4). The hearts of those who care for them must be turned toward the hearts of children with compassion, humility, gentleness, and patience. This is supported by the CRC. It also legally obligates a country to embark upon programs that will enable parents to fulfill their responsibilities as dictated by the convention. As a result, more than 95 percent of the world's children now live in states obligated by law to protect them.

Political and Economic Realities

And you will hear of wars and rumors of wars; see that you are not alarmed; for this must take place, but the end is not yet. For nation will rise against nation, and kingdom against kingdom, and there will be famines and earthquakes in various places: all this is but the beginning of the birth pangs. (Matt. 24: 6-8)

For the mystery of lawlessness is already at work, but only until the one who now restrains it is removed. (2 Thess. 2:7)

Currently there are few places on earth that more accurately reflect the above passage from Matthew than the African continent. The cropping up of crisis after crisis has seriously impeded efforts toward what one likes to call normality. What Paul calls the "secret power of wickedness" spoken of by Paul in the second passage, has increased in intensity, resulting in political and economic confusion and a seemingly total disregard for moral standards and commitments.

Educational opportunities, occupational responsibilities, and daily activities are limited or impossible because of wars, damage to the environment, or the breakdown of law, order, and government. As a result large numbers of people are left idle, unemployment has soared, cities have become overcrowded, crime has increased, and disease has become rampant. In a vicious cycle of poverty and neglect, children have lost their innocence and become victims of a world that accords them few rights and no control.

Foreign Aid No Panacea

There seem to be both inability and refusal by some African leaders to formulate policies that make the best use of their countries' natural resources and support their human populations. As a crowning blow, it is widely believed that external aid has, if anything, made bad situations worse. One thing is clear: financial assistance has not produced self-sustaining economic growth. Nor, over the past decades, has it prevented the collapse of numerous poor societies. And always, always, the children suffer most.

Despite the vast monetary and human resources that have been poured into foreign aid, the desired levels of economic growth have not been achieved. Nor has such aid fostered the development of democratic institutions. Furthermore, it is known that private agricultural lands have been confiscated by governments in efforts to increase their export production. The victims? Women and their children, since apart from government farms, women are the predominant food producers in Africa. The result? They are left with the poorest land and diminishing annual yields, drastically reducing the domestic food supply.

It has been suggested that the unwillingness of African leaders to execute policy reform has to do with their desire to stay in power, on the premise that too much change could be political suicide. In many cases, foreign aid allows them to cover up problems, delay reforms—and ultimately be driven into the seeming morass of structural adjustment. If we are to have an intelligent understanding of these matters, it is crucial that we have at least a minimal working knowledge of policies underlying the current situation in Africa—a situation that determines the fate of Africa's children. One of the most controversial of these policies is "structural adjustment"—administered by the World Bank and the International Monetary Fund (IMF); designed to pressure borrower countries to earn the foreign exchange needed to service their debt repayment.

In 1987, "Adjustment With a Human Face," a survey by the United Nations Children's Fund (UNICEF), found that in many countries under structural adjustment there had been an increase in the number of poor people. The availability of food per person had declined in more than half of the countries that received adjustment loans between 1980 and 1987, and there was a general deterioration in child welfare during the same period as efforts toward children's health were damaged and their chances at education reduced. [29]

Two years later in its annual report, *The State of the World's Children,* UNICEF called the 1980s "the decade of despair." The report revealed that in the twelve months prior to its publication, a million young children in the developing world had died because of a slowing down or reversal of progress in their regions. [30]

Nevertheless, it is clear that structural adjustment cannot be blamed for all that is awry in African states. Development cannot occur in the absence of a healthy, enabling environment. Africa is the only region in the world in which poverty is expected to increase during the coming years. Too many countries are struggling with civil strife, overpopulation, a largely unskilled and impoverished population, heavy debt burdens, and minimal investment flows because of poor business climates. [31]

Learning to Govern

Because of the styles of governance in many African countries, the line between political and economic matters is often razor-thin. As political systems developed, so did the belief that he who held the power also controlled the purse. Even today, political and economic power have become so entwined that they are inseparable. Hence, their joint treatment in this section.

God's purpose in government is to give humans laws by which they can rule themselves in righteousness and justice. All leaders are under moral obligation to use power and influence for the good of government and of all people in their charge (Rom. 13).

The African leaders who came to power immediately following independence had high ideals and great expectations for their respective nations. They believed that their dreams of industrialization, economic growth, and international standing were about to come true. However, there was no consensus about the meaning of independence. Though they were perhaps naive, they believed themselves capable and ready to overcome the legacies of colonialism and to compete in a global economy.

Much emphasis was placed on nation-building. Colonial borders had been permanently fused into nation states with disparate groups and interests. Eager for an administration unlike that of their former colonial masters, many leaders leaned toward a socialism based on an African model that they believed was similar to traditional governing bodies and would take grassroots interests seriously.

It didn't work. Personalities got in the way, the masses became distrustful, and the growing suspicions of other leaders hindered the desired cooperation. African socialism as a political ideology failed. Efforts to form regional blocks and economic unions did not fare much better, although in

1963, representatives of thirty nations assembled to form the Organization of African Unity (OAU) in an effort to promote unity and solidarity among its members through various cooperative means.

After initial attempts to form some type of governing strategy for their nations, most leaders settled for administrations structured around a major political party, or a one-party state. It was thought that by concentrating the decision-making in the hands of a few, the process of bringing about change would be hastened. This could have worked, but not everyone in government had the good of the masses at heart. Thus, the lack of control without political opposition enabled bribery and corruption to flourish on a wide scale. Disgruntled groups reacted with bloody ethnic clashes, each protesting the lack of justice and equal representation. Still, the more the political process evolved, the more autocratic the governments became.

There is a saying in Africa that people get the leaders they deserve. More to the point, too many African leaders have chosen to follow after strange gods, rejecting good counsel and paths leading to prosperity, and doing little or nothing to reverse the deplorable conditions that exist in their states.

Effects of the Cold War

During the Cold War era, authoritarian governance worked to the advantage of various western governments who sought allies on the continent, seeking to forestall the communist threat. The foreign allies aided and propped up these regimes and in some cases even manipulated internal events in order to aid friendly puppet governments.

These western "friends" turned their backs as the leaders became dictators, brutally abusing every imaginable form of human rights, entrenching themselves in the seats of power, and depositing western monetary donations into personal foreign bank accounts. Dictators such as Mobutu Sese Seko of Zaire (now the Democratic Republic of Congo) and others amassed huge personal fortunes in the billions of dollars even as their populations faced abject poverty and starvation and the infrastructure of their countries went into shameful decay.

Seemingly, the goal was to remain in power as long as possible by any means possible. Intimidation and torture became the order of the day, as fear was instilled into the minds of everyone. Personal militias, special armored divisions, and presidential guards sustained the power of the dictators by carrying out reigns of terror. All important positions in government were given to relatives, fellow tribesmen, and other loyal supporters. Constitutions were amended or suspended in order to eliminate clauses limiting the length of time one could remain in office and to give a free hand in matters of governance. (Many African leaders have been in office for more than thirty years. Few have resigned on their own. Even after being ousted by the military or in democratic elections, some have tried to return to the seat of power.)

Opposing factions or individuals were declared "enemies of the state," and were frequently forced to flee for their lives. Intervention by the military to curb government corruption and inefficiency was at first warmly welcomed by the general public. However, only rarely did the military fulfill its promises—especially that of stepping down after order had been restored!—and most became ever more brutal and dictatorial, propped up by the power of the gun.

When the Cold War ended, so did western support for many African regimes. By 1985, most were turning to the World Bank and the International Monetary Fund, accepting, at least in principle, programs of structural adjustment.

Personal Observation

By the time we arrived in Zaire, Mobutus' brainwashing of the general populace was almost complete. Our friends and neighbors were so afraid that they actually believed Mobutu could hear what they said even in the privacy of their own bedrooms. We were told stories of how they would stand for hours or dance for hours in the blazing sun or pouring rain when Mobutu or one of his henchmen was to be in town. I asked why they didn't go home, since the arrival time was continuously pushed ahead. The reply was always that they were afraid! Mobutu went as far as banning Christmas and other Christian holidays and replacing them with his wife's birthday and other Mobutu holidays. His mother was referred to as "The Virgin Mary." Yet, he was declared a friend of the United States and for many years received U.S. support. . . .

[Eventually] the banks failed. People who had money in them lost everything. All the money was on the street in the black market. We would take our dollars there to exchange for zaires. The exchange rate was so low for zaires that the bills were tied and counted as "bricks" rather than as individual bills. Even so, I often went to the market with a shopping bag full of zaires and came home with a small basket of goods.

Economic Growth: Hopes and Fears

According to African Development Bank estimates, nearly half of the continent's 760 million people are what is termed "profoundly poor," that is, surviving on less than one dollar per day. This presents an enormous barrier to the rearing of children in a modern society.

As suggested earlier, it has been extremely difficult to impose economic reforms from the outside. Many Africans responsible for economic reform in their countries do not believe they are able to compete in the world market, and that pulling down import barriers and forcing them to go head-to-head with countries like Korea or Argentina would devastate many of their home-grown industries.

As for privatization, such industries often end up in the hands of foreigners because few African businesses have the resources to compete for them. The investors may stay in the background, with a local person to front for them, but the bulk of the capital, and, therefore, real ownership, ends up in the hands of outsiders, usually—as has recently been the case—Lebanese or East Asians.

Donors now conclude that the solution to economic growth is "ownership," that is, having African governments accept responsibility for economic reforms in their countries. This would allow them to tailor reforms to their individual economic environments. They have established the three following criteria: 1. the development of a strong technocratic cadre that has the confidence of the political leadership; 2. a political leadership with self-confidence in its dealings both with internal interest groups and with external financiers; 3. sufficient political development and stability that the government is free to pursue long-term economic goals.

Foreign Investment and Jubilee 2000

Foreign investment continues to shy away from Africa because of weak financial sectors, poor infrastructure, unskilled workers, political instability, stifling bureaucracy, unpredictable legal and regulatory systems, and corruption. The United States government made some efforts to help African nations through a variety of economic arrangements, but Congress is still adamant about an end to human rights violations and a number of other issues.

Many in the United States believe that the best way to help Africa is to forgive billions of dollars in loans that various countries owe the United States. Church World Service and Witness, in honor of its Jubilee 2000, endorses a worldwide movement to cancel immediately the crushing international debt of impoverished countries. The benefits of debt relief, according to CWSW, would include saving "21 million children from disease and hunger in Africa".[32]

Throughout the Scriptures, there are examples of the need for sympathy toward those who have suffered setbacks or experienced circumstances which brought them into poverty or debt. As we pray, asking God to forgive us our debts as we forgive our debtors, we must realize the implications and extent of those words, and be willing to act as true followers of Christ [see also Deut. 15:1-5].

Having said all of that, however, it must be reiterated that African governments have a serious responsibility to make changes that will improve their economic prospects, and, thus, the lives of their people. Most importantly, without security and without the structures in place that will prevent a return to war, neither economic reform nor political stability can be realized.

The Church Stands Strong

Nevertheless, given the opportunity, Africa's citizens can bring about the economic turn-around needed to ensure their future. The church—specifically The United Methodist church—has through its associations and partnerships in Africa come to realize the great potential of Africa's citizens, who have proven that even under conditions of dire poverty, their individual initiative has brought about change. Perhaps this change is too small for consideration by governments whose policies are geared toward much larger groups. However, it has also been demonstrated over time that government policies failed because group expectations were too complex.

Personal Observation

Serving as educational consultant for UMC schools in Nigeria afforded me the opportunity of witnessing at first hand the benefits of partnerships. As Nigeria's partner, the Iowa Conference is the largest supporter of education in Nigeria. Over the years this conference has financed the building of new facilities and the renovation and modernization of existing ones; has subsidized nutrition programs; and has sent various experts to conduct teacher-training and leadership-training workshops.

The needs were great and populations to be served were extremely large and scattered over hundreds of miles. Often we felt overwhelmed, but the State Board of Education assured us that our institutions were far superior to any existing in that region. We were getting the job done! Our only regret was that at some point we would have to abandon our students to an education system that thrives on bribery and corruption with no opportunity for fair competition based on earned grades (university level). Though we were deeply concerned about our inadequacy for preparing students for the world outside UMC schools, we are convinced that the basic Christian values of honesty and hard work, instilled in them on a daily basis, would carry them through.

Not only are individuals easier to work with than groups, but they promise much better returns in whatever investment is made. No one can deny that cottage industries and cooperatives work in most parts of Africa, but rarely do governments tap such potential for economic turn-around. Also, it is known that, in general, women, including illiterate women, are better managers than men. Furthermore, it has been shown that relief is more widespread if handled by women, because they have been conditioned to think in terms of children and families.

Personal Observation

Nearly all the women of the former Central Zaire Annual Conference [now the Central Congo Annual Conference] are farmers. Less than five percent can read and write, yet they have an incomparable dynamism when it comes to the church. Their activities have become so widespread and diversified that they hold their own mini-conference during the annual conference.

Each area raises funds in highly competitive fashion, the women doing creative scheming to raise their contributions. During one annual conference, the women of Lodja area forged ahead and to their great surprise raised the largest funds. They were ecstatic—dancing and jubilating because they had put the others to shame. Later we discovered their secret. Since the value of the zaire fluctuated daily—mostly downward—Elaine Crowder, a local missionary who held their purse, had wisely converted their treasury into dollars. By the time of the conference, although the dollar amount was less than five dollars, its new conversion value in the local currency had multiplied by millions of zaires. All the women learned a valuable financial lesson in that deeply impoverished region that would mean much as they saved for the coming year's school fees and other necessities.

African Leadership and Economic Growth

Throughout Africa, answered prayers have resulted in what is being called a "new breed" of leaders. There is encouraging evidence that economically and politically things are changing. Political liberalization and, in some countries, even the conflicts have given rise to a new generation of leadership. This group, while admitting that Africa still needs help, believes that Africa can and must shape its own future.

The change in leadership style is noticeable. The old authoritarianism is giving way to more liberal (even if not democratic) styles of governance. Efforts are being made to include well-educated technocrats as government advisors. There is still a serious absence of strong opposition parties and structures which can limit excesses of power by those in top positions. Still, there are those of us who choose to believe that the emergence of various civic and professional associations, public interest groups, and a free press will serve as stepping stones toward the development of a political climate dedicated to economic progress.

In the international community, the economic forecast for Africa has already changed. Growth is small but steady. Eleven countries have maintained rates of over seven percent between 1990 and 1997: Angola, Benin, Botswana, Equatorial Guinea, Ethiopia, Guinea Bissau, Ivory Coast, Lesotho, Mauritius, Togo, and Uganda. When examined regionally, Africa's growth will always be negative. However, when looked at country by country, positive growth—though small—is evident.

Some leaders are figuring out how to use their natural and human resources advantageously. They have learned from past failures and are adamant about giving their regions a new start. A recent *Time* magazine article, featuring the initiatives of the following African countries—initiatives that have given hope to their populations—struck an optimistic note:

> Out of sight of a narrow focus on disaster, another Africa is rising, an Africa that works: the Africa of Mozambique and Mali, of Eritrea and Ghana, of South Africa and Uganda, Benin and Botswana, Ethiopia, Ivory Coast, Tanzania.
>
> What's new is how some nations are figuring out ways to harness their resources into working models of development, even while others cannot. What's new is the astonishing extent to which ordinary Africans are searching out their own paths to progress. What's new is how much of the still limited prosperity and security they have managed to acquire is homegrown—political and economic advances rooted in the soil of local culture. What's new is that the enduring example of Nelson Mandela has heartened all Africans with a fresh vision of leadership, of how men of their own kind can be admired, respected, even emulated.
>
> —— Johanna McGeary and Marguerite Michaels, "Africa Rising," Time, p. 35.

Although in most of these countries the statistics still show abysmal levels of poverty, illiteracy, and early mortality, they are recording higher growth rates, lower inflation, and more stable currencies. The authors point out that the new initiatives have yet to trickle down to those most in need. However, we must at least recognize the potential for growth in the light of our purpose in this study. Given the enormity of the problem, the scarcity of domestic and international financial resources, and a lack of proven alternatives, there are reasons to feel encouraged and filled with a sense of hope.

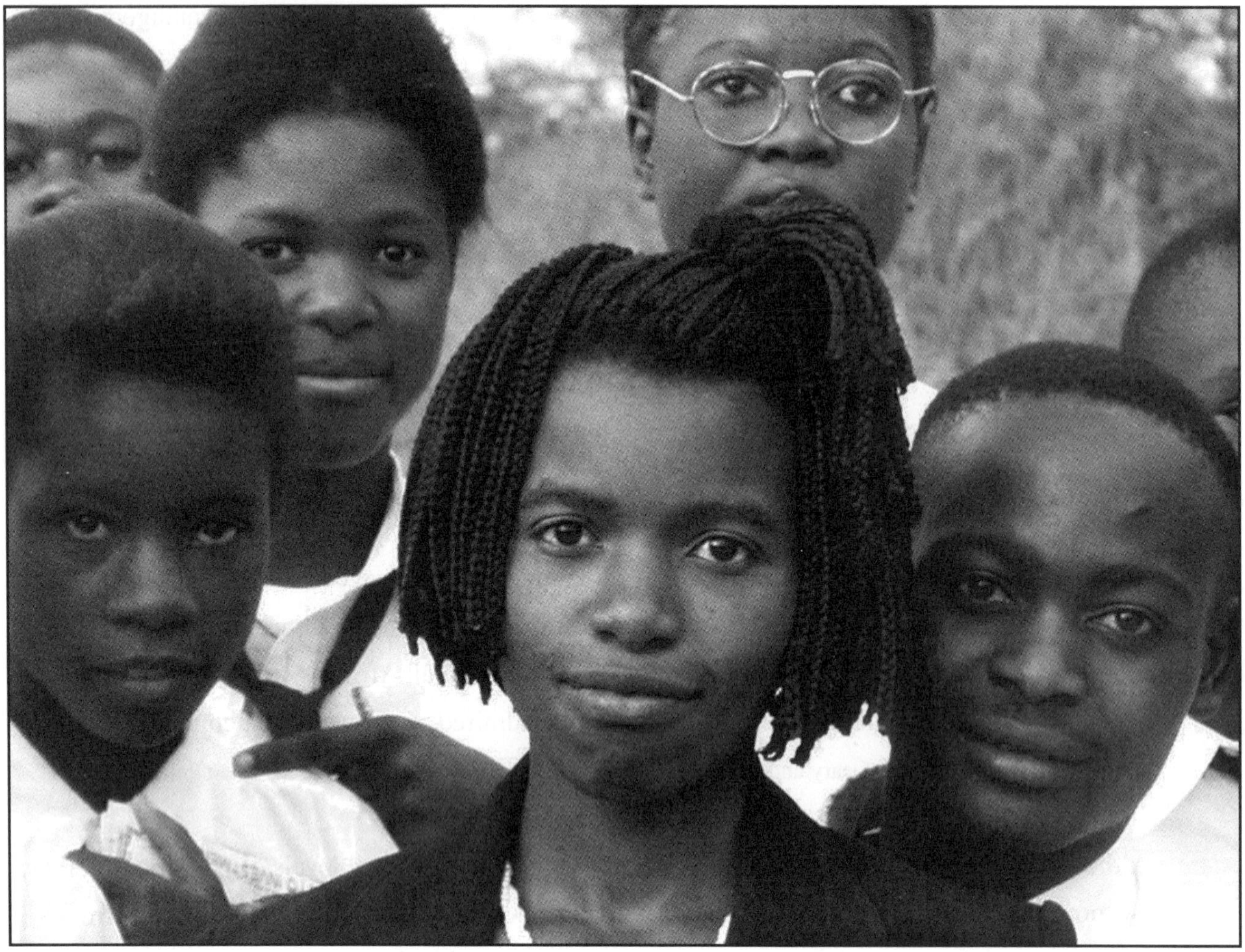

6

The Church in Africa: Source of Caring, Courage, and Hope

Christianity in Africa: A Historical Perspective

Christianity has a long-established history in Africa. The Egyptian Coptic Church dates back to the third century and claims to have learned about Jesus from St. Mark himself. By the beginning of the fourth century, parts of the Scriptures had already been translated into several of the region's non-Greek languages; Christian churches were active in such cities as Carthage and Tunis, and, generally, throughout North Africa.

The monastic tradition sprang up in Egypt during the third century. Christian hermits lived in villages and devoted themselves to lives of prayer and contemplation. The southward spread of Christianity into present-day Sudan and Ethiopia began in the fifth century. These churches grew so strong that Christianity became the prevailing faith in the region, though in the sixth century there was a waning of the Christian faith as Islamic missionary activity became intense. Although Christianity suffered setbacks in the four centuries between 950 and 1350, a sizable majority of Christians managed to hold on to the faith.

The period of European exploration added new dimensions to the spread of Christianity. On the surface, justification for establishing colonies in Africa seemed humane: Africans were to be brought out of savagery through economic development and the spread of Christianity. It was seen as a civilizing and Christianizing mission. The earliest missionaries came under the auspices of colonial governments for the purpose of serving the colonial populations. Only later did they begin to assist in the conversion of Africans to Christianity. As the colonial powers entrenched themselves politically and economically, the church soon became identified with the larger motives of territorial acquisition and a desire for minerals, agricultural products, and markets, nullifying any benefits for African populations as these were stripped of their territories and their rights. In the unforgettable words of Jomo Kenyatta: "The Africans had the land and the Christians had the Bible. They taught us to pray with our eyes closed. When we opened them, they had the land and we had the Bible."

As exploration and colonization progressed, so did the work of the missionaries. The first arrivals were Roman Catholic, but between 1800 and 1900, especially in sub-Saharan Africa, Protestant missionaries far outnumbered the former. As a result of the conversion of various tribal groups, Christian communities sprang up along the African coast. American Methodism came to Africa in 1823 with the arrival of Daniel Coker, a black Methodist minister from Baltimore—one of a freed group of slaves from the United States. Throughout the next century, the predecessor denominations of The United Methodist Church sent missionaries to the regions known today as Algeria, Angola, Democratic Republic of Congo, Liberia, Mozambique, Nigeria, Sierra Leone, Tunisia, and Zimbabwe.

The impact of Christianity in sub-Saharan Africa has been debated from both negative and positive perspectives: Negative in that, based on ideas of European racial dominance, it did not promote a positive African identity, requiring, rather, absolute obedience to the political system, and resulting in loss of land, natural wealth, and power to the colonial masters. On the positive side, the struggle against imperialism owes much to Christianity's impact upon Africa. There were many missionaries who fought slavery and did much to help bring it to an end. They developed written forms of expression for tribal languages and translated the Scriptures into local dialects. They were the first to bring western medicines into the continent. They built and maintained the vast majority of schools seeking to prepare Africans for a world dominated by European education and mores.

Christianity, particularly its significant efforts in education, provided the impetus for the first wave of African nationalists. It has been suggested, interestingly, that mission education helped develop global awareness, enabling Africans to challenge some of the basic assumptions of the time. For example, if all of humanity was created and loved equally by God, there could be no rational justification for colonialism. So, while it is true that Christianity was often an ally of colonialism, it was unquestionably a partner in liberation.

> At the Eighth Assembly of the World Council of Churches meeting in Harare, Zimbabwe, Nelson Mandela singled out the work of missionary teachers who worked in South Africa when he was a child. "My generation is the product of church education," he said. By contrast, he said, the government of his day "took no interest whatsoever in educating Africans, people of mixed race, or Indians."
>
> His remarks were recently seconded by a prominent African on the subject of church-sponsored schools. In November, Kofi Annan, Secretary General of the United Nations, received the World Methodist Peace Award, and in response he favorably recalled his education in a Methodist school in Ghana. He said he was fortunate to have had teachers "who understood the value of knowledge infused with a moral purpose."
>
> —— Gustav Niebuhr, *The New York Times*, Dec. 19, 1998, p. A12.

Other African nationalists who are products of mission schools include Kenneth Kaunda (Zambia), Jomo Kenyatta (Kenya), Robert Mugabe (Zimbabwe), Kwame Nkrumah (Ghana), and many others among today's African heads of state.

Missions of the numerous African Methodist conferences also attest truthfully to the positive impact of Christianity on their regions. Today, as in the past, the mission tradition of United Methodism continues to help bring about spiritual and material advancement in many parts of Africa. The United Methodist Church has more than 800,000 members in twelve sub-Saharan nations. These are organized into three central conferences—West Africa, Congo, and Central Africa—led by African bishops. Furthermore, the General Board of Global Ministries of The United Methodist Church has relationships with autonomous Methodist churches in Ghana, Ivory Coast, Kenya, Nigeria, and South Africa. Methodists in these churches number at least half a million.

The newest conference, the East Africa Annual Conference, is also growing rapidly as churches in Burundi, Kenya, Rwanda, Sudan, and Uganda reach out to recent refugee populations. Today, as many as 30,000 persons worship in United Methodist churches throughout Rwanda. Although most of them are Hutu, in the capital, Kigali, there are congregations in which Hutus and Tutsis worship together—an indication that the seeds of reconciliation may be starting to grow.

The early missionaries gave permanent roots to Christianity in Africa by winning converts and recruiting and training them to lead churches and carry on the faith. Though they came from far away, the relevance of faith in Jesus Christ permeated the African existence early on, is undergoing a revival, and is fulfilling spiritual aspirations. Africans find confidence and hope in the gospel, expressing the wonders of God as only they can, in worship and prayer. When such expressions are in their own dialects, Jesus Christ becomes a reality in the tongue of the heart: the mother tongue. It is an astonishing and remarkable truth that African Christians constitute the fastest-growing church in the world today.

The African Church: An Agent of Change

The African church has proven itself to be a formidable factor in the struggle for African solutions to African problems. It has stood the test of time as an institution of hope and trust, and now leads in the process of peace, justice, and liberation across the continent. Over the years, as Africa vacillated in its attempts toward growth and prosperity, the confidence of its people in established institutions and systems failed. Time and time again they were let down by political, economic, social, and environmental institutions only to be faced with armed conflict, ecological disasters, and ethnic strife, as well as increased poverty, malnutrition, and disease. As regime after regime reneged on promises, the church became a symbol of stability and trust.

It was so in the refugee camps of northern Zaire [now the Democratic Republic of Congo] as churches became the rallying point, offering comfort, a sense of dignity, and spiritual guidance. Among those fleeing was a group of Christians who had already begun relating to the United Methodist Church. Soon their number grew to 20,000. The UMC joined hands with African church leaders as well as other NGOs to set up schools, care for orphans, provide food and clothing, and develop a sense of community. Later, thousands of Africans were cared for by United Methodist medical teams. When war broke out in the Democratic Republic of Congo, it was a United Methodist superintendent, Pastor Kuberuaka Jupa, who led the refugee congregation back to Rwanda.

Student pastors at an institution in Burundi—Mweya Bible College (which was totally destroyed)—were also among those who fled, and were able to continue their studies in the area of the camps on UMC scholarships. They were given the responsibility of serving as teachers in several of the primary schools set up for children in the camps. The United Methodist Church also took the lead in Sierra Leone's recent conflict, its youth setting up classes for children inside the country as well for those who had fled to Guinea and other places. This was an important way of engaging the children and restoring a sense of normalcy and purpose in their lives.

Members of African churches dig wells, provide roads, and help rebuild homes in areas that have suffered disaster. They provide other essential services, especially health care. Increasingly, as government hospitals and clinics deteriorate, the church is called upon to shoulder the responsibility of caring for the sick. As conflicts end, it is to the churches that people flock for assistance. Societal problems such as AIDS education and drug rehabilitation are all challenges that have been taken on by the church in Africa. Increasingly, men and women have been enriched and sustained by the power of the gospel, believing that through the hand of God they will overcome all obstacles and survive.

Africans are, in general, a deeply religious people. Even traditional beliefs have at their center the concept of a Supreme Being: the creator god who in times of trouble will intervene in the lives of human beings and bring them safely through crises. Now that Jesus Christ has become the vital force in the lives of millions of Africans, it should not be surprising that the church in Africa is growing so rapidly. Neither should it be surprising that in these turbulent times it would stand out as that one certain refuge offering both spiritual and physical relief. The African churches are in the forefront, pressing for peace, political transformation, and reconciliation. Two Mozambican church leaders won the first All-African Conference of Churches Peace Prize. In Sierra Leone and Liberia, United Methodists are assisting in the establishing of peace and reconstructing of the environment. UMC bishop Tilewa Johnson played a notable role in Gambia as the chairperson of the electoral commission. In Kenya, the churches serve as advocates for a new constitution. It was the religious community that assisted in meetings that helped to ensure a bloodless takeover from Mobutu in Zaire.

In spite of the way in which the world looks at Africa, Africans themselves have no doubt that the future belongs to them. They will not be ignored or left out. They are, first of all, encouraged by the fact that their populations are very young. Estimates suggest that more than 60 percent of Africans are under twenty-one years of age. Those under fifteen make up 50 percent of the population. These young people are the hope of Africa. Already they have caught the vision; already they have joined in the struggle for peace, justice, and progress.

Another promising factor is the abundance and diversity of the continent's wealth. Wise management of these resources under democratic forms of government, together with complementary economic and social systems, can ensure unlimited possibilities for a promising African future.

A third factor is the faith of the African people. They say that they are troubled but not destroyed; that they may be scientifically and technologically backward, but the rest of the world cannot succeed at reconstruction without them. They are determined that the many crises facing Africa will not divide them. The believe that if they and their leaders humble themselves before God, they will be empowered. Allegiance, they say, should no longer be based on a broken witness manifested by denominational trivialities, and they are prepared to embark upon any type of work that will help them demonstrate their Christian convictions.

—— Adapted from "Challenges and Hopes in Africa Today" (Excerpts from speeches of Archbishop Desmond Tutu and Jose Chipenda at the General Assembly of the All-African Conference of Churches)

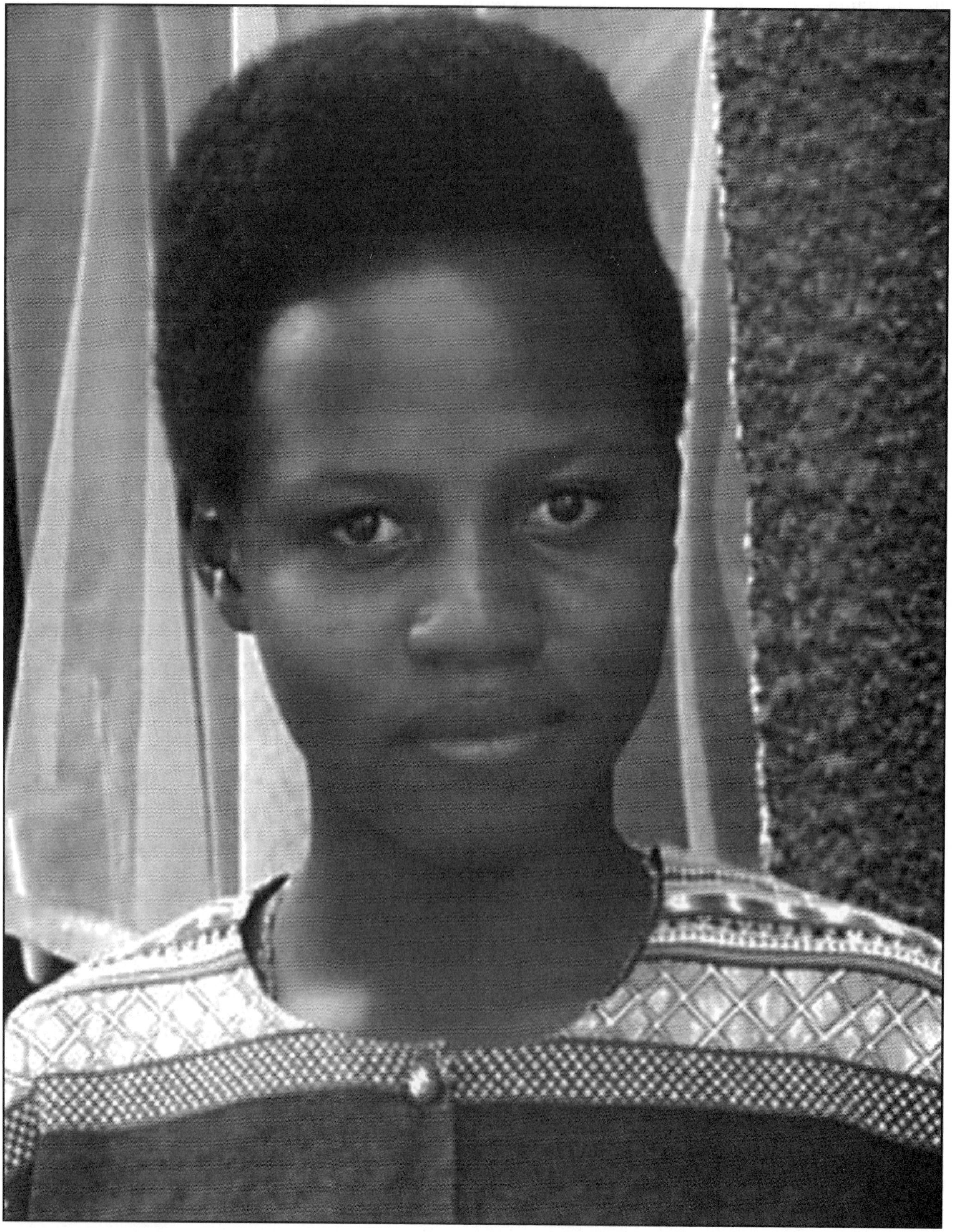

7
We Are All Part of the Global Village

<u>The Global Village</u>

The concept "global village" expresses the reality that the world has become a network of interconnecting and interdependent realities. No longer can nations or individuals stand alone or choose an isolationist course, because outside the network there can be no progress—perhaps not even survival.

The concept grew out of workshops sponsored by the All-Africa Conference of Churches. Its symbol is a village with a baobab tree in its center. The village represents an inclusive community under the direction and guidance of God. Within, reside all the positive traditional values of African society. The baobab tree is within the village, standing for continuity, dialogue, sharing, clarifying of issues, and learning and teaching within the community. Thus, the global village is an inclusive community in perfect harmony—with God and its own traditions. Its hopes and aspirations are for the continued health and welfare of all who live in the village. And change is brought about equitably, through dialogue, discussion, and teaching—without strife or conflict. Every success or failure, joy or pain, is shared, since all are contributors and partakers.

The Meaning of the Village Concept
- It is a circular process requiring a commitment by both individuals and the community as a whole.
- The individual must work for the community. Everyone has a role to play, and the community has responsibility for the full development of each individual.
- Full development includes not only spiritual development, but also social, economic, and political development.
- It is an inclusive community that counts as its members all people within the society: the young, the elderly, women, men, Christians, and non-Christians.
- Each individual in the community, regardless of who she or he is, is recognized as the creation of God, as someone who has been blessed with unique gifts.
- It acknowledges the gifts of each human being, and challenges each individual to offer those gifts to improve the life of the community. In the process the individual is empowered, nurtured, and fulfilled.
- It relies on participation. This includes not only acting, but also listening and sharing. Each form of

participation in the life of the community is regarded as equal in value—a condition that challenges present attitudes and practices of clergy, Christian educators, and laity alike.
- Through dialogue, the participants share unique personal insights in order to come up with new ideas and solutions for communal problems.
- The "village" is not a geographical location. It is a concept. As such, it is also used as "village church," "village nation," "village continent," "village world," and "village community."
- It offers opportunities to integrate worship, evangelism, Christian education, women, youth, development, and communication into one unified witness.
- Because the theology, liturgy, and hymns of the church in Africa are largely imported, it also offers the church an opportunity to develop its own distinct identity.

Thus, the concept of the village speaks to the desire of African Christians not only to assert their African-ness, but also to take part in a process of wholistic growth with others and with Christ. An overarching goal is to make Africans aware of the fact that they are an essential part of the global village and, therefore, must contribute to its life.

We, too, are part of the global village; one contribution made by the United Methodist Church is its Mission Intern Program and those who offer their skills and services. This program offers to young adults opportunities to develop leadership skills as they participate with Christian communities around the world in the search for justice and empowerment. The program includes fifteen months of work-study in an assignment outside the United States, and sixteen months of action-education somewhere within the United States. Applicants must be committed to the gospel of Jesus Christ and willing to live at the level of the community in which they serve.

Amy Peel of Orlando, Florida, has experienced the global village concept as a UMC mission intern in Johannesburg, South Africa. She worked primarily with pre-school children in a program called FLOC (For Love of Children). This program, designed for poor children in Johannesburg, is funded in part by the Women's Division of the General Board of Global Ministries, The United Methodist Church. The following excerpt is from a letter that Amy wrote to the GBGM about her work:

> The children are the delight of my days and a symbol of hope that this country will be able to start again. My major responsibilities include chapel time for the children, weekly Bible stories, staff devotions and individual work with children and staff. . . . I am also helping to integrate an anti-bias/peace education curriculum into the classroom. This has been incredibly exciting and

inspiring! The teachers are a close-knit community of women, with whom I do a lot of interacting. . . . I feel truly blessed to be welcomed into their lives. . . ."

The local director of FLOC made the following comments in a letter to Amy: "We greatly appreciate the contributions to our project and want you to know how invaluable they are. It is also heartwarming to be connected with the United Methodist Church. We are truly a worldwide family."

Every Child Is Our Child

"Whose child is this?" the General Board of Global Ministries asked at the 1997 Global Gathering, and heard the resounding response, "God's child—and all our children." As the mission agency for a global church, the General Board of Global Ministries is actively involved in improving the quality of life for children around the world.

The United Methodist Church in its *Book of Discipline* asserts that the rights of children are food, clothing, shelter, health care, and emotional well-being. No longer are children to be considered the property of parents, but must be acknowledged as full human beings in their own right, to whom the general society has specific obligations. For the African child, these rights are affirmed by The United Methodist Church through its large number of programs in the following categories:

- Church outreach: day care, after-school, camps, tutoring and mentoring, drug prevention
- Health: immunizations, maternal and child health, community clinics, the environment
- Hunger and poverty: nutrition, shelter
- Issue education: resources on abuse, violence, war, substance abuse, and others
- Legislation: voter registration
- Mission education: Vacation Bible School
- Special initiatives concerning children and youth: Bishops' Initiative on Children and Poverty
- Special funding: projects supported through committees on national and international ministries with women, children and youth

African children have benefitted greatly from the special funding category. Nearly all African conferences have received or will receive funding directed specifically toward children for some basic need. The following are examples:
- Angola West: *UMC Day Care Center, Viana*—funding to support children's programs in the nursery, and for street children
- Angola West: *UMC Youth Department*—funding aimed at alleviating poverty, unemployment, vio-

lence, and for the advancement of education

- Angola East: *UMC Quessa Orphanage, Melange*—funding to provide books for refugee orphans
- Benin: *MC Center for Education in Nutrition*—funding for the purchase of materials and supplies for maternal and child care needs of women and infants in the Dangbo region
- Kenya: *MC AIDS Awareness Program*—funding to support AIDS prevention among youth
- Liberia: *UMC Day Care Center, Monrovia*—funding to provide food for children
- Mozambique: *UMC Chicuque Hospital*—funding to provide assistance for prenatal, maternal, and pediatric programs at the Cambine hospital and clinic
- Mozambique: *UMC Women's Desk Program Centers for Shelter for Abandoned Children*—funding to support these safe havens for children abandoned because of war
- Sierra Leone: *UMC Nursery School, Moyamba*—funding to support the school's health and education programs
- South Africa: *EMSENI Community Center Project*—funding to provide basic education for fifty deprived children

Africa at the Crossroads: Bishops' Appeal and Campaign: Hope for the Children of Africa

Hope for the Children of Africa is a five-year effort to raise extra gifts for extraordinary times. It has the following aims:

1. To provide relief and reconciliation for thousands of children and families who have suffered and sustained great losses because of wars throughout the continent

2. To rebuild United Methodist churches and restore ministries, with special attention to the physical, social, and spiritual well-being of children

The programs fall under the following four categories

1. Health of children
2. Education of children
3. Children of war
4. Social, emotional, and spiritual nurture of children

The Bishops' Initiative on Children and Poverty is an effort to confront the social, economic, political, moral, and spiritual concerns that cast a growing number of people—and especially children—into poverty.

In Gisenyi, Rwanda, there are now forty children in a small community. They have no parents, and those who are lucky are cared for by an extended family. These children are receiving housing and education partly through the gifts of other children in Onondoga Hill UMC near Syracuse, New York. Pastor Jupa, wanting more for these children, and with the help of local children, began to build a house and educate them.

——— Bishop Forest C. Stith, "Children Helping Children in Rwanda."

It was the young people of Onondago Hill UMC, when learning of the UMC's faith journey in Rwanda, initiated the effort that led to a major project in that area. The children here gave and the children there built, all for the effort of our global village. "As the Council of Bishops leads the church in the Campaign for Hope for the Children of Africa," says Bishop Stith, "we need to remember that these issues are not abstract, but real and concrete, in the lives of children."

Action Plans for U.S. Congregations

As has been noted throughout this study, The United Methodist Church is actively involved in God's mission of love, justice, and compassion for the people of Africa, especially children. The UMC's efforts are realized chiefly through the support of its local churches, that is, groups and individuals just like ourselves, who comprise the various congregations nationwide and throughout the world. As we internalize this study, let us consider some of the many ways in which all of us can share in this mission for the children of Africa:

- **Support World Service** and other apportioned funds and conference benevolences that undergird all mission programs of The United Methodist Church, including those that are related to the children of Africa.
- **Encourage Your United Methodist Women's Unit** to fulfill its pledge to mission that supports projects related to children all over the world.
- **Give to "A Child" (Advance #123456-3)** if you want your gift to be used in any specific capacity for children in Africa.
- **Select a Specific Project** from the *Advance Book of Children's Projects*, which outlines all United Methodist Church projects related to children in various African countries.
- **Give through "The Advance for Christ and His Church,"** an official second-mile channel that offers an opportunity to turn your gifts into exciting ministries. One hundred percent of each gift goes to the project of your choice.
- **Develop Educational Exchange Programs** for teachers and students.

Become a Partner Congregation or Conference by supporting a project from the *Catalog of Advance Specials*, which includes the following:

- *Africa Church Growth and Development* funds church construction, scholarships, Christian education and evangelism efforts, bicycles, and other projects related to African churches. (#008233-0HT; #008235-2AT)
- *The Bishops' Appeal or the Hope for the Children of Africa Fund* provides relief and reconciliation for the victims of war, with special attention to the health; the education; and the social, spiritual, and emotional nurturing of children. (#101000-4)
- *The Bishops' Initiative on Children and Poverty* seeks to address the social, political, economic, moral, and spiritual concerns that cast a growing number of people—especially children—into desperate need.
- *Global Refugee Response Program* provides assistance to uprooted people (refugees, asylum

seekers, and the internally displaced) around the world. (#982540-1)

- *World Hunger/Poverty Program* responds to the nutritional needs of children worldwide, and has been especially instrumental in providing food for children in Africa. (#982920-4)
- *Global Mission Partners* allows your church to support a missionary commissioned by the General Board of Global Ministries, and to support a person in mission named and sent by a partner church to serve in his/her own country. (012122-6GL)
- *Missionaries Outside the United States* allows the GBGM to recruit and commission missionaries to serve throughout the world. As part of this program, a congregation may establish a covenant relationship with a missionary couple or an individual. (#000779-6HZ)
- *National/International Persons in Mission* helps partner churches fulfill critical needs by making available funds that can be used for salaries, training, and other vital needs.
- *Shared Mission Focus on Young People* provides opportunities to help develop dynamic new ministries with young people throughout the world. (#194790-2)

UMCOR Advance

This program makes possible direct ministry to persons in need through programs of relief, rehabilitation, and service, including help for refugees as well as responses to hunger, poverty, and disaster.

- **I**nvolve Your Sunday School in the Medicine Box Appeal, a program filling immense needs as societies try to regroup after armed conflict.
- **Support Girl-Child Education** through The Forum for African Women Educationalists, P.O. Box 53168, Nairobi, Kenya. Tel. 254-233-0352; Fax: 254-221-0709.
- **Support the Education of a UMC Child** through the various projects of the Women's Division of the General Board of Global Ministries' International Ministries on Women, Children, and Youth.
- **Become a Volunteer in Mission** with the added bonus of sharing in mission first-hand.
- **Establish Networks with Missionaries** serving in countries and with work experiences that are of particular interest to you. This might (though not necessarily) entail a covenant relation ship and include a visit.
- **Organize a Work Team** to visit a specific destination for a brief period for a specific project agreed upon by you and the receiving conference.
- **Provide Bibles and Tracts** for African young people who under ordinary circumstances would never have the opportunity to own either.
- **Help Fund the Salary of a UMC Teacher** in one of the many UMC schools throughout Africa.

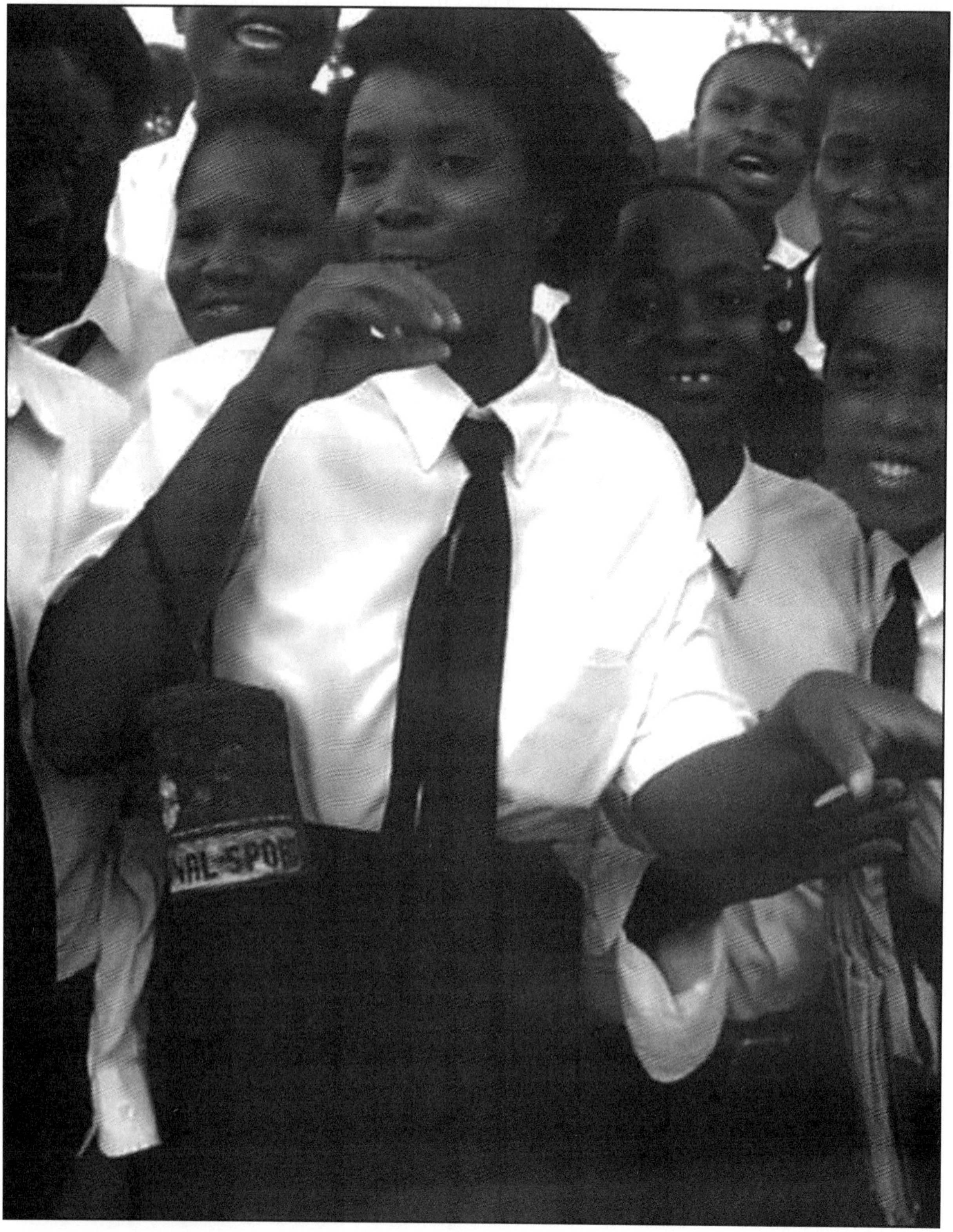

- *Provide Scholarships for Village Youth,* especially those orphans whose fathers were UMC pastors.
- *Establish a Nutrition Project* and choose the annual conference that will receive your funding.
- *Fund the Digging of a Well* in an area that has serious water problems and where there is not already an established wells project.
- *Become an Advocate,* expressing your concern about various issues relating to African children by writing to one or more of the following:
 1. Your representative in the United States Congress
 2. U.S. Secretary of State Madeline K. Albright, State Department, 2201 C. Street, N.W., Washington, D.C, E-mail: secretary@state.gov. (stating your concerns about relevant U.S. policy)
 3. Church World Service, P.O. Box 968, Elkhart, IN 46515, Tel: 219-264-3102; Fax: 219-262-0966 (for information about ways to support development in Africa)
 4. Bread for the World, 1100 Wayne Avenue, Suite 1000, Silver Springs, MD 20910, Tel: 310-608-2400 (for an update about advocacy related to development aid or foreign aid)

Other Initiatives
- *Operation Classroom:* A project of the Indiana Conference that offers support for UMC schools in Sierra Leone. To contact, please write to Operation Classroom, The United Methodist Church, 207 West Jackson Street., P.O. Box 277, Colfax, IN.
- *Volunteers in Mission:* United Methodist conferences or churches in the United States can form a VIM team to go to a destination in Africa for a limited period in order to help with specific, focused projects: repair or construction of buildings, and a large range of other services. Arrangements for such a trip can be made through Volunteers in Mission, General Board of Global Ministries, New York, NY.
- *Africa University:* Located in Mutare, Zimbabwe, Africa University is the first institution of higher education established by The United Methodist Church on the African continent for the purpose of educating students from countries throughout the continent. For further information about how you can help Africa University and its students, contact James Salley, Development Officer for Africa University, Board of Higher Education, Nashville, TN.
- *All-Africa Women's Desk:* This is part of the All-Africa Conference of Churches. For information about projects sponsored by this desk, please contact Battu Jawambai, Women's Desk, All-Africa Conference of Churches, Nairobi, Kenya.
- *Women's, Children's, and Youth Desks of African Annual Conferences,* or other Methodist national church offices are other excellent sources for information about what support you can lend.

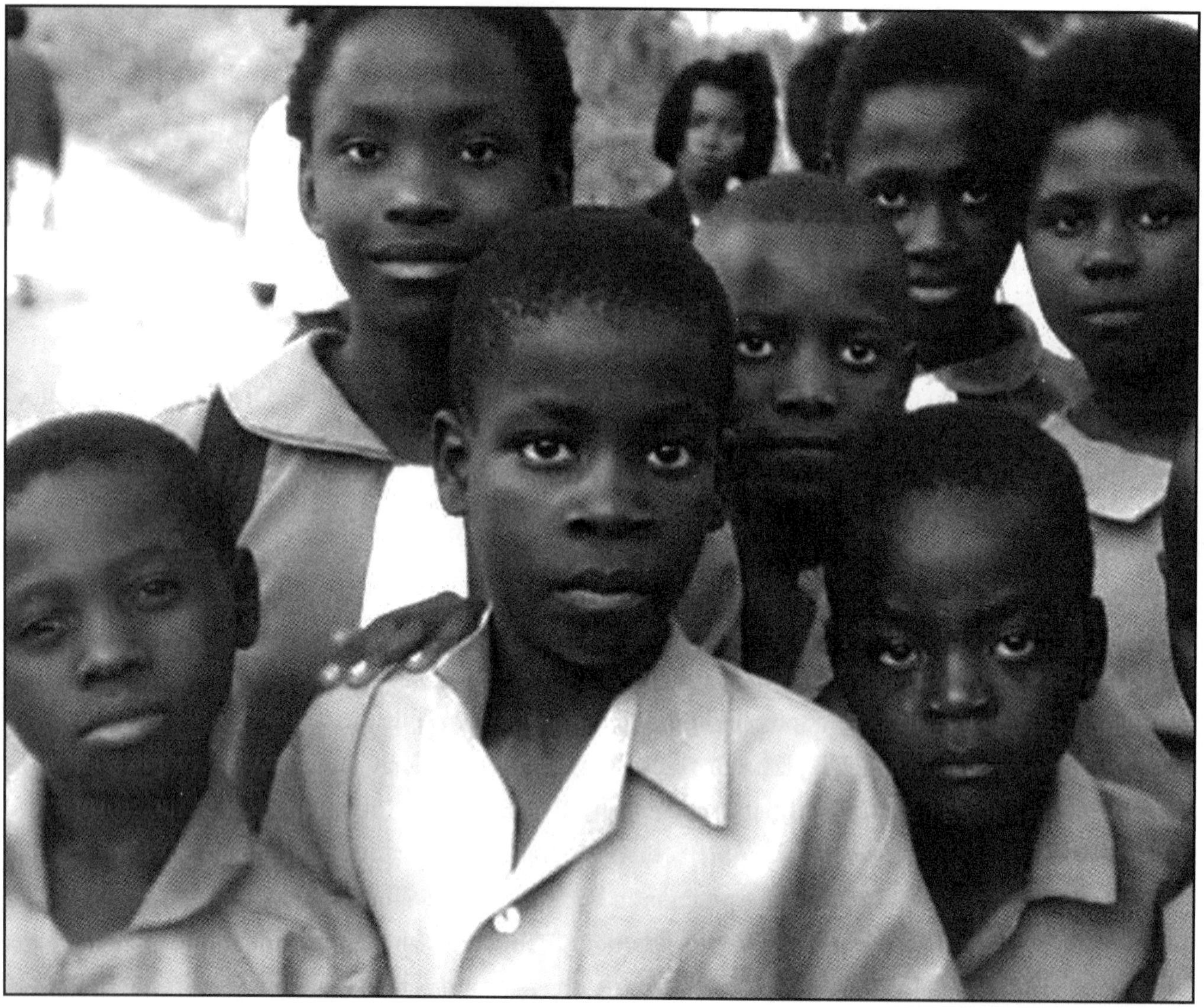

Children of Africa

Leaders' Guide

by
Anne Leo Ellis

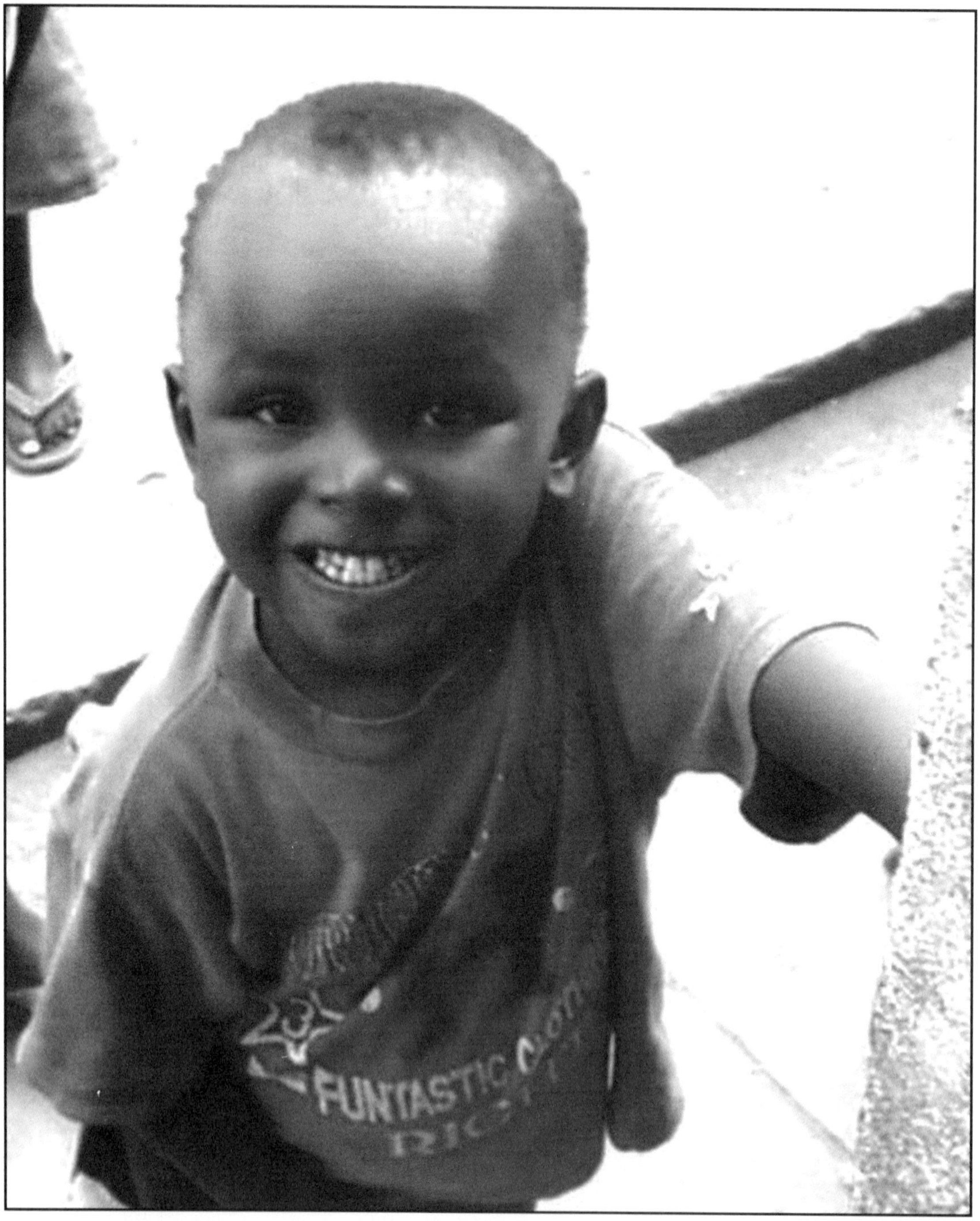
FUNTASTIC

Contents

Introduction 74

Session 1: Children at Risk: Good Health and Nutrition 80

Session 2: Armed Conflict and the Destruction of Childhood 86

Session 3: The Shattered Lives of Forgotten Children 92

Session 4: Education, the Healer; Decisions of Nations: Their Impact on Children 99

Session 5: The Church in Africa and the Global Village 108

Introduction

Welcome to this study of children in Africa. As writer of this guide, I am delighted that you have chosen to be a leader, and hope you will find the experience fulfilling and productive. I also hope that this guide will be helpful, as you and your group work with Jackie Onwu's fascinating and disturbing book.

Children of Africa concerns itself with some of the harshest societal issues in the world today. Although it is a book that will demand much of you and your study group, it will be worth your time, your energy, and your commitment. In spite of the many visual images all of us have seen, and see almost every week, of distressing situations in Africa (floods of refugees, children with assault rifles, homeless orphans, to name a few); and in spite of the many news stories we read about these situations, this study will make significant demands upon the imagination of you and your group: namely, the ability to connect seriously and productively with another realm of existence as real as our own.

Jackie Onwu's book presents its readers with an unsparing picture of the current situation in many African countries: political and economic policies; conditions of armed conflict, both internal and with other countries; approaches to the health and education of their citizens; the appalling problems that currently afflict millions of African children; and what is being done by a variety of groups from within Africa as well as other parts of the world—including the church—to address these issues.

The leaders' guide suggests reading brief extracts from Onwu's book and occasional other sources, and attempts to help you and your group examine them closely through questions for discussion, suggestions for further reading, and various interactive activities and exercises. If you have participated in mission studies before this, you may be surprised that there is little role play or acting-out of skits. Much of the material seemed not to lend itself to such tools. Why? It was hard to visualize adult group members acting out the traumas of children. And it seemed, in this particular instance, to trivialize the seriousness of the subject matter. As a result, there may be more discussion and direct examination of issues than might otherwise be the case. And, although that may place a greater burden on you, the study leader, the fascination of some of the discussions should make up for that.

It is important to mention that this is a very straightforward examination of current situations in African countries. Although it is about children—because they are currently in the most serious difficulty—it is not the kind of sentimental glimpse that we are all familiar with. Both basic book and leader's guide call upon participants to move beyond emotion to serious examination of underlying problems, and how they are being/can be addressed.

In addition to questions and aids for study of the material, the guide includes a number of litanies and prayers, as well as Bible passages for biblical reflection. You will find a list of appropriate hymns at the end of the guide. Please feel free to use these or to prepare/choose your own. It is my hope that it will help you and your group explore the wealth of material in the basic book, and let it become a part of each group member's thinking.

Currently, many of Africa's children find themselves in desperate straits. Because of political and economic turmoil, millions of children are being subjected to conditions not a single one of them should be forced to experience. Such conditions are the unhappy result of many interwoven strands: armed conflict, internal displacement, poverty, disease, hunger—situations that many African nations are struggling to solve with greater or lesser success.

Children are affected perhaps more directly than anyone. For the youngest, it is the only reality they know. For the older, a former life has been wrest from them, and they are powerless. Often they must watch the helplessness and despair of their parents, as well. Or, they must make their own way without parents. No society can flourish if its youngest and most vulnerable members do not have the opportunity to grow and mature in a supportive environment. And, according to Onwu, such a supportive and loving environment was, until not so long ago, a given in the lives of Africa's children:

The world of the African child has always ensured a very safe and secure existence. The foundation for this security is a basic belief that children are unique beings endowed with special qualities based on God's divine order. In Africa, children are regarded as very close to God, lent to parents, but still under God's watchful eye, and engaged in a relationship with God that is different from their relationship with adults. They were part of their families before they were born, since it is believed that the attributes of loved ones who have left this life will be regenerated in new individualsl.

As community life retained and constantly reshaped the modes and morals of public behavior, everyone in the family and the village was responsible for the upbringing of the children. Nurturing abounded in acts of love, patience, and kindness designed to foster an environment friendly and responsive to the development of well-brought-up and well-disciplined children. Everyone in the community strove to make each individual child achieve maximum potential in an area of its own capacities and inclinations, because individual achievements were also communal achievements.

— Onwu, p. vi

During a time in which many African societies have been thrown into disarray by wars, famine, chaos, and inadequate systems of governance, such stable and loving arrangements have all but disappeared for large numbers of Africa's children. This tragic situation is the focus of our study.

While by no means all African children live in poverty and despair, even the most fortunate are affected in some way, as we can learn by reading the report of children from a school in West Cape, South Africa, who speak up for the rights of the African child [Onwu, chapter 5]. However, millions live in conditions that should not be tolerated: children forced to put in long hours of labor; children with AIDS; children forced into prostitution for a variety of reasons; children without enough to eat, without sanitation, without homes, without schooling, without a future; children engaged as soldiers in one armed conflict after the other. Sensitive internationalists have provided us with the UN's excellent document, "Convention for the Rights of the Child," but although most countries have signed, its provisions have yet to become reality for most of the world's children—including those in many African countries.

What do we do? How can we help? The United Methodist Church is already engaged in many creative ways, and they will be discussed in Session 5 of this study. However, a very first step, as we begin, is to familiarize ourselves with the vast continent of Africa, if we have not already done so. Take the time with your group to review a map of Africa. (Be sure that there is a large, clear map of the continent in everyone's line of vision at all times.) Ask group members to locate on the map the countries mentioned by Onwu. Assign volunteers to research something distinctive about each of these countries, and to share that information with the group. Many Westerners need to remember that the people of Africa are no more a monolithic society than are the people of Asia or Europe or Latin America. In each region there are great variations in culture and ethnicity. However, although most Americans have some idea of the difference between Norway and Italy, Japan and India, Brazil and Mexico, how many of us know some of the distinctions between Mali and Morocco or Niger and Namibia? As for geographical knowledge: How many of us can point to Ghana or Zambia or Ethiopia or Botswana or Mozambique?

Encourage the members of your group during and between these study sessions to think about

Africa and to learn something about its richness and variety of culture as you all struggle with the study's main focus: Africa's children, their present reality, and their prospects for the future. Ask your group to think of these children in their difficult, often intolerable, situations, as if they were children in your own communities. It will help lessen the gulf between our two societies, help bring the predicament of these children closer, and make their plight easier to comprehend.

Also remember that during the very time of this study about Africa's children there is much in our own society that needs healing as we all, here and abroad, seek to build safer and better societies for our children—our future.

A final note: In the words of Bishop J. Alfred Ndoricimpa of the East Africa Annual Conference, "The sound of Africa is not just the sound of war. It is the sound of children playing and laughing. It is the sound of people singing God's praise. It is the sound of hope." This is important to remember. We want, even as we study the very hard and tough parts of some African children's lives, to recognize that laughter, joy, music, gentleness—even playfulness—are so much a part of African life. In each session we have allowed for an activity centering on that truth. We have included some children's songs and games, as well as hymns, in the Appendices. You and your group may wish to use these and build them into your study sessions. Then, at the end, perhaps you may wish to have an celebratory African evening with characteristic African foods (look for a page of recipes in the Appendices.)

As Leader, Plan the Study Well in Advance

- Leave yourself plenty of time to read and absorb Jackie Onwu's book, *Children of Africa*. It is crammed with important information, and you will need to know the material well enough so that (using this guide as an aid) you will be able to outline a study that will be right for your group.
- There will be times when you may not be able to cover all of the material, so you will need to make choices—or feel free to let it run over into the next session.
- Be sure to use input from your group members, who may be able to supply a gold mine of personal experience, observation, and information.

General Preparation for All Sessions

- Tools: Have available at each session
    a. Large map of Africa
    b. Easel with large sheets of newsprint or a chalkboard

c. Black magic markers/chalk
   d. Map'n Facts #2875
   e. Bulletin board
   f. Good 1-volume dictionary (for ex.: *Merriam Webster's Collegiate Dictionary*, 10th ed.)
   g. Good 1-volume encyclopedia (for ex.: *Columbia Encyclopedia*, 5th ed.)
   h. Good map in book form (for ex.: *Hammond Explorer Atlas of the World.*
   i. Bible

- Country Cards. Before the first session, write the name of each African country mentioned in Jackie Onwu's book on a separate index card and distribute one card to each participant (if necessary, make several cards for one country). Let each person assume personal responsibility for keeping abreast of issues relating to that country, remembering that country and its people in private and group prayer, and bringing information, news, pictures, fabrics, or art objects from that country to share with the group. If a specific country will be dealt with, ask a volunteer in advance to prepare a brief presentation of that country.

- Journal. Suggest to group members that they keep a journal of what seems important to them during the coming sessions: matters that encourage or discourage them, that they regard as profound or notable, or that they particularly wish to remember. During the final session, set aside time for the reading and discussion of journal extracts for those who would like to share them with the group.

- The Internet. If you do not have Internet access at home, call your library, church, college, or computer friend. They will be happy to help. If you are not familiar with computers, find someone in the group to be the class "computer guru." Chances are, that group members will be only too happy to print out for the class relevant study materials available on a variety of Africa-related websites.

Preparation of Meeting Room
- Arrangement of chairs: A circle, semicircle, or concentric circles usually convey openness and community, and encourage active participation. Chairs with attached writing surfaces will enable participants to take notes and balance books more easily. If the group is small, you may wish to be seated around a table. In all cases, allow sufficient open space for movement and activities. The least desirable setting is a room with immovable seats, such as an auditorium or sanctuary.

- Comfort: Be sure the room is large enough for the number of people you expect—with room for movement and comfortable room temperature (and that you know how to adjust it). Check the location of rest rooms and notify class in first session.

- Teaching Environment: Try to create a setting that is inviting and appropriate to the content of the study. Display pictures and posters. If possible, put up a bulletin board or large sheet of paper on a wall for the display of magazine and newspaper clippings. You may wish to use distinctive African fabrics in some way to add character and context to the setting. Be sure to have either chalkboard and chalk, or an easel, newsprint pad, and markers. If you plan to use audiovisuals, be sure to locate the outlets, have a three-prong adapter and extension cord, and check out how to darken the room. Position the screen or video monitor where everyone can see, and make sure that all equipment is in good working order. (If possible, try out everything in advance to avoid unhappy last-minute surprises.)

[Text or ideas adapted, with thanks, from Ruth A. Daugherty, Toby Gould, and Peggy Halsey from their study guides, respectively, for *John Wesley: Holiness of Heart and Life; The Bible: The Book That Bridges the Millennium; and Family: Drawing the Circle Wide.*]

Devotions for These Sessions

Each session begins with one or several scripture passages. You may wish to use these in a brief opening devotion. It might be best for you, as leader, to be responsible for the opening session. After that, ask for volunteers. Remind them that they need not use the same format each time, nor do they need to use the suggested passages. They may wish to choose passages of their own. Likewise, they may wish to use the prayers and litanies in this leaders' guide or prepare their own. Remember, also, the listing of appropriate hymns at the end of the guide.

Preparation for Session 1
Reading: Chapter 1, *Children of Africa*

Session 1: Children at Risk: Good Health and Nutrition

Jesus called for them and said, "Let the . . . children come to me; and do not stop them; for it is to such as these that the kingdom of God belongs. (Luke 18: 15, 16)

"Then he took a little child and put it among them; and taking it in his arms, he said to them, 'Whoever welcomes one such child in my name welcomes me, and whoever welcomes me welcomes not me but the one who sent me." (Mark 9: 36, 37)

Brief Opening Worship

For this first session, it would be appropriate for you, as leader, to prepare a brief opening worship, using, if you wish, the scripture passages above, the prayer below, and hymns selected from the hymn section in the Appendix. You might ask volunteers to do this in coming sessions. Remember, also, that there are several African hymns in the United Methodist Hymnal *and in the General Board of Global Ministries' collection of hymns and songs from around the world,* Global Praise I.

Gracious God. We thank you for the privilege of assembling for this study of Africa's children and of the problems in today's Africa. Help us to see the people of Africa—indeed, of all the world—as part of our lives, part of our responsibility—because we are all members of your human family. Help us approach our study with humility, knowing that we, too, have societal problems and lack answers to many troubling questions concerning our own youth. Give us the strength to take what we learn during the following weeks and put it to good use, so that we may in some small way help to improve the lives of Africa's children. We ask it in the name of your son, Jesus Christ. Amen.

Welcome to this Study

Begin the session with a welcome to your group. Ask each person to introduce him- or herself. Spend some time in conversation; ask each person to tell the group why she/he chose to attend this study and what he/she hopes to learn from it; try to discover how much participants know about the current situation of children in Africa, and about political and social developments on the continent. Find out if persons in the group have direct experience with Africa. Are there missionaries; former members of the Peace Corps; anyone else who has traveled or worked in Africa? Are any group members African by birth? If so, in what countries were they born? If there are such knowledgeable people in the group, they can serve to enrich the study in many ways.

The following questions provide much material for exploration of the issues. Please, as leader, add your own. Also, ask the members of your group to suggest questions and topics for discussion. Always encourage the inclusion of current material from the news or other sources (make use of the bulletin board!). Arrange study sessions in a way that is most compatible with your group: a) frame discussions for the whole group point by point; b) break up into groups of 3 or 4 people, leaving time at the end for the sharing of conclusions or interesting results with the whole group; c) break into small groups for part of the session, and reconfigure the groups for further discussions; or, d) other techniques that seem comfortable and appropriate. Ask small groups to choose one or more of the questions below, or to address their own further questions. Use a chalkboard or an easel with large sheets of newsprint, as well as Bible, dictionary, or encyclopedia (See "General Preparation for All Sessions" in Introduction).

Objectives

- To become familiar with members of the group
- To examine a map of Africa
- To discuss in general terms the scope of the entire study
- To learn about the desperate need for children's health facilities throughout Africa
- To examine the connections between lack of safe water and a host of health-related problems as they affect children
- To understand the reality and the reasons for Africa's current scourge of AIDS, and its troubling ramifications for the future

Introduction to Session 1

Before plunging into the heart of the study, take time with your group to examine a map of the African continent. (Beginning with this session, prepare tiny tags to be fastened to the map with tape or push-pins, identifying the places where specific things mentioned in the text have happened/are happening. Try to have a large map in a place where all members of the group can see it easily. Or, consider distributing blank maps and ask group participants to try filling in the names of countries. Also, call their attention to the map on the inside cover. Take some time to discuss at least those African countries with which most persons have some vague familiarity, as well as those you will be discussing in this study. This session introduces your group to many African children's lack of health care and nutrition, basics that most Westerners take for granted. *If at all possible, ask participants to read chapter 1 in Onwu's book before this first session.*

1. Clean, Safe Water

Analysis (Read about water-borne and sanitation-related diseases in Onwu, chapter 1.)

Nearly everywhere throughout Africa there is a need for clean, safe drinking water, affecting every facet of life. Bacterial and viral diseases contracted through the drinking of contaminated water include cholera, typhoid, childhood diarrheal ailments, infectious hepatitis, and poliomyelitis. Drinking water may also be contaminated with parasites causing river blindness and guinea worm, in which ingested larvae mature internally, eventually bursting through the skin.

Exercise

Make a list on the chalkboard or newsprint of the many kinds of diseases that are the result of polluted water. If you need more information, consult your encyclopedia. Make another list of the kinds of activities that lead to such pollution, such as bathing in, doing laundry in, and drinking the same river water. How can such and other practices be overcome?

2. Malnutrition

Analysis

In Mali it is estimated that 3.3 million people suffer from malnutrition, including 25 percent of children aged 3 months to 3 years. Even in Egypt, more than 12 percent of children under age 5 are malnourished. . . . Hunger is a complex problem and one that is amplified by its constant companions: poverty and disease. Worldwide, the combination of these three devastating conditions has a profound and debilitating effect on more than 800 million lives.

—— Whiteside, "The Answer to Hunger's Root Causes—Development,"
New World Outlook, Jan/Feb 1999, p. 18.

For Discussion

Discuss the worldwide blight of malnutrition. How is it a local or a global problem? Why is it that malnutrition is rarely regarded as an emergency? What, exactly, is malnutrition? What are the signs? How can it be avoided?

Exercise

Ask one group member to list on a chalkboard or newsprint the group's suggestions of the ways in which malnutrition manifests itself, physically as well as psychologically. Make another list of the kinds of diets that may lead to malnutrition in the situations we are studying. Discuss ways in which action of African governments might help to overcome childhood malnutrition.

3. AIDS

Each day 5,500 funeral ceremonies are conducted as a result of AIDS. "And the worst is yet to come," predicts Agathe Latre-Gato Lawson, the United Nations AIDS (UNAIDS) representative for Ivory Coast."

—— *Le Figaro,* Paris, Nov. 25, 1998, [Onwu, chapter 1]

For Discussion

Onwu writes that the AIDS epidemic has left in its wake devastated villages, decimated families, and tens of thousands of orphans. Discuss in your group what happens to these children, particularly if they are also infected. Try to imagine the situation of one family. What are the prospects for such children if both parents die?

Exercise

Ask someone in the group to read the two following pieces: the true story of Akwatura and the imagined monologue that follows. After the volunteer finishes reading, let another volunteer ask the questions below, with time for reflection after each one, as a kind of meditation without open discussion. Close with prayer. Perhaps you may wish to go around the circle and let those who wish add phrases to a closing prayer related to what they have just experienced in the readings.

> At 57, the widowed Akwatura is raising seven young children orphaned by AIDS, four of them her own grandchildren and three others—two one-year-olds and a two-year-old—

abandoned and suffering from malnutrition. 'I am proud to be able to look after these orphans', Akwatura says. 'I can feed them properly and I am pleased that the older ones are going to school and doing well.'"

———— Meldrum, Andrew. Guardian News Service, London,
World Press Review, Nov.1997, p. 42. *[Onwu, chapter 1]*

Monologue
This takes the true story of Akwatura (above) as its point of departure, but everything else is imagined. Perhaps it could be read to the group by a volunteer and used as a springboard for further discussion.

I just visited Akwatura. I wanted to cry, and I did. She's such a strong, wonderful woman, and she just took me in her arms and comforted me. When I consider what she's been through, and what she's doing! Husband dead and two of her children dead. So she's taking care of four grandkids. And then she took in three more when her neighbors died last year. Seven children she's taking care of! Seven! I can't believe it. And she's not young. She must be at least sixty! And she certainly isn't rich.

All the kids' parents had that terrible disease. And now I've got it, too. Akatura was looking at me. I could tell she was shocked. I hadn't seen her for ages. She could see I'd lost weight. My skin looks so unhealthy, and I feel weak all the time. The baby's due in three months, and what am I going to do? I haven't got energy for anything. The last three times I was pregnant, I felt strong as a tiger! To the moment of delivery. Everyone couldn't believe how much energy I had!

And then my man took that other woman. And then another and another. I don't know what got into him! I know he's allowed more wives than one. I never liked the idea, but what could I do? But after a while I could tell something was happening. He didn't act the same. And I could tell he wasn't well. I asked what was wrong, and he told me not to ask silly questions. Nothing was wrong. Nothing! But I knew better. And when I look at him now, I know he won't be around much longer. Then what am I going to do? Four small children, if this one I'm carrying even lives, and no husband. And now he's made *me* sick, too! What's going to happen to my babies when I die? How many Akaturas are there? *She slumps over in despair and exhaustion.*

After the volunteer has finished reading the monologue, allow a few moments of silence while people think through the implications of what they have just heard. Then let the volunteer ask the following questions (and others, if she/he wishes) while group members listen and think about them.

- What is the response of most of us to such human need? What is my own response to homelessness and poverty in our own society?
- For too long, Africa has been in denial about the reality of AIDS. What is my own response to any disease in others that I believe—perhaps unjustly—has been brought about by a lifestyle of which I disapprove. Am I judgmental or caring? What should be my response as a Christian?
- Do I, as someone living on the other side of the world, have a responsibility to help people like Akatura's friend? If yes, what should I do? Should I give money or worry about U.S. aid to Africa, or what? How can any one person help with such a huge problem?
- I shudder to think of myself in the position of Akatura's friend. She seems so strong, but she's utterly helpless—completely dependent. How can women/men like me help women—not only in Afghanistan—who are completely at the mercy of men who regard them as chattel? What about the situation in my own community; my own church?

Closing Prayer

Exercise: Songs and Play of Africa's Children
Somewhere during this session you may wish to insert a bit of child's playfulness: a children's song, a game—something that will provide some insight into the life of an African child in lighthearted moments (which usually exist even in the midst of all the harshness) and provide a break for group members and strengthen them for the tough stuff ahead. It's a good psychological tool and may make the study that much more effective. There are several children's play songs in the appendix, which would be easy and fun to sing, as well as some games. Perhaps the games may be best for reading only (unless you have a very energetic and playful group!) Remember, also, that the recipes in the appendix can lay the groundwork for an African festival at the end of your study.

What *We* Can Do
Ask group members to begin thinking, already, about what hands-on things they can do to help children in Africa—both individually after the end of the study group and right now, as a group. Ask them to examine the listings in chapter 7 of Onwu's book, and in Session 5 of this study guide. What would be good things to think about doing and then actually following through?

Two Brief Prayers from Africa

For a Peaceful Night: O God, you have let me pass the day in peace; let me pass the night in peace, O Lord who has no lord. There is no strength but in you. You alone have no obligation. Under your hand I pass the night. You are my Mother and my Father. Amen.
(Traditional prayer of the Boran people, *The United Methodist Hymnal*, p. 692)

For the Spirit of Truth: From the cowardice that dares not face new truth, from the laziness that is contented with half-truth, from the arrogance that thinks it knows all truth, Good Lord, deliver me. Amen.
(Kenya, *The United Methodist Hymnal*, p. 597)

Preparation for Session 2
Reading: Chapter 3, *Children of Africa*
Ask for a volunteer to prepare a brief opening worship for the next session.

Session 2: *Armed Conflict and the Destruction of Childhood*

Brief Opening Worship
For opening worship, the volunteer may wish to use the Bible passage and prayer below, as well as hymns from the United Methodist Hymnal and a selection of African hymns in the appendix. Note, also, the litany at the end of this session.

> *He shall judge between the nations, and shall arbitrate for many peoples; they shall beat their swords into plowshares, and their spears into pruning hooks; nation shall not lift up sword against nation, neither shall they learn war anymore.* (Isaiah 2:4)

O God, help us during this session, indeed, at all times, be sensitive to the enormous, sometimes unimaginable evils of this world. Let us not resist knowing that children—not only in Africa—are being mistreated and abused; that often those closest to them have neither the strength nor the resources to resist the forces that plunge their children into disaster. Give us the discipline and the commitment to learn about such things and to determine what we can do to help, be it with our money, our time, our efforts at advocacy, or whatever means available. Be with those children in Africa about whom we will learn more today, who, even as we pray this prayer, are hungry, are ill, are being kept in ignorance, are forced into giving their bodies and their souls to evil purposes. Be with them, O God, and give them the strength to survive. Amen.

Objectives

- To learn about the growing scourge of child soldiers; why children are being used in this way; what can be done to stop it
- To become knowledgeable about the ongoing horror of land mines—and to understand how the United States continues to be implicated
- To recognize the connections between Africa's devastating armed conflicts and such ills as child prostitution; masses of orphaned, displaced, and homeless children; and the realities of disease and hunger

Introduction to Session 2

In this session (and the next) members of the study group will focus on the terrible reality of life for many African children in countries torn by war and internal armed conflict. Difficult as it is, group members need to move beyond compassion to tough analysis, and discussion of causes and solutions. We shall also discuss what we can do to help. Remember as you do this study, that in Section 5 there are listings of and information about what the United Methodist Church is doing—and how group members can connect (many will already have done so) with such projects.

A. Child Soldiers

Vignette of a Former Child Soldier *(Read in Onwu text, chapter 3.)*

Exercise

Divide into two groups. Let one group discuss the increase of violence in Africa: what effect it has on young people; what the effect on the future of Africa may be. Let the other group discuss violence among young people in the United States: from inner city to suburbs. Let the groups come together and exchange information and ideas. It may seem unlikely, but if there are any similar strands, what are they?

B. Orphans

By the end of 1884, Rwanda had more than 100,000 displaced children, and by 1995, UNICEF reported that 20 percent of Angola's children were separated from their parents. What is the fate of these children? What can/should the global community do? Is anything being done?

Exercise

On a chalkboard or newsprint make two lists: a) steps taken by the international community with Kosovar refugees; b) steps taken by the international community in situations such as the Rwanda refugee crisis. What are the similarities? What are the differences. Give reasons why. Discuss the world's attitude toward Africa's displaced children.

Exercise

Divide the group into two or more small groups. Discuss the following statement by Onwu: "A society that mobilizes and trains its young for war, weaves violence into the fabric of life, increasing the likelihood that violence and war will be its future." How is this similar to U.S. concerns? Make notes of your conversations and share them with the whole group. Leave time for conversation about the groups' findings.

C. Land Mines

Onwu writes that the land mine is a small metallic or non-metallic device which requires very little pressure to detonate. It comes in two types: blast and fragmentation. Blast mines cripple or kill by the upward force of the explosion. Fragmentation mines spew pieces of hot steel that penetrate and tear. Mines are laid individually by hand, dropped mechanically, scattered from helicopters, or fired in bunches from artillery and rockets. They may remain active for up to 50 years. In Africa the mines have been randomly placed, often around schools, water sources, individual homes and agricultural lands, as well as along roads, at border points, and around military bases. [Onwu, chapter 3]

Vignette

Children are among those most at risk because frequently their daily activities such as collecting firewood, fetching water, grazing animals, even engaging in outdoor play, become high-risk and potentially fatal activities in areas littered with landmines. Rae McGrath, director of the Mines Advisory Group, tells of an incident which, while not in Africa, could have happened in any landmine-infested rural situation:

> "I was examining the site of a mine incident . . . where a six-year-old boy had died. The boy had strayed into a minefield while playing, but it was not clear at all how he could possibly have stood on a mine accidentally; the mines, all-surface laid pressure devices, were clearly visible, and it was unlikely that the boy, from a village in a heavily-mined area, would not have recognized them as mines. The area was grassland meadow, and it was only when I crouched to inspect the accident site that I suddenly realized why the boy had died. Although the grass was no more than six inches high, from my new position I could see no mines. I could only see grass. My eye level was roughly that of a boy of six. The victim died because he was too small."
>
> ——— "Landmines: Fallout of War," CWSW, reprinted in *New World Outlook*,
> Jan/Feb 1997.

Vignette

At the first All Africa Disaster Management Training Course, Mary Salesa Ondoga of Uganda [held up a handmade doll with rounded hands and feet, and] said "I chose this baby from the play-therapy suitcase. She is like the children I see in my work—children who do not have hands, fingers, toes, and feet—victims of landmines." An estimated 300 million landmines are present on African soil and more continue to be planted. They are weapons of war used not to impede armies but to intimidate civilians and maim unsuspecting victims. Many such victims are children who forage for food or for sticks of firewood.

——— Adapted from Weaver, "Disaster-Management Training in Africa,"
New World Outlook, Jan/Feb 1999, p. 35.

For Discussion

Children are often more directly affected by the presence of land mines than adults. Try to imagine a situation in which the terrain in which children live and play is planted with land mines. How are land mines disrupting daily life? What is required to clear the land of the mines? Try to imagine the havoc, uncertainty, and fear that grips a community in which one dare not take an unconsidered step without risking an explosion. A terrible statistic in Onwu's text is that in Angola, which is said to have the world's highest number of amputees per inhabitant, there are 70,000 amputees, of whom 8,000 are children. To recognize the unspeakable horror of such a statistic, and bring it close to home, try to imagine a similar situation in your own community or state.

What We Can Do

Ask two volunteers each to read one of the vignettes above. Then engage the group in a discussion about current anti-landmine efforts throughout the world. [See Appendices]. Ask the group to write letters to representatives and officials in Washington to encourage U.S. signing of an international ban of antipersonnel mines. If so, have writing materials ready to distribute. This will be a major group act of advocacy.

Exercise: Songs and Play of Africa's Children

If you wish to do this exercise, remember that it can be inserted wherever you think best. It serves as a powerful reminder that the children discussed in this session have been robbed of their childhood. Remember to check out the songs and games in the Appendices. Perhaps a volunteer would like to choose and present the song and/or game. Or perhaps a group of volunteers might want to sing a song for the group or demonstrate a game. Take a few moments to plan your African feast, if you are planning one at the end of the study.

Litany

We pray for young boys pulled into the terrors of warfare and killing, that they may survive both physically and spiritually.

> *We ask it, O God.*

We pray for young girls and boys forced into prostitution. Make it possible for them to move beyond the present into a better future.

> *We ask it, O God.*

We pray that young children will not be spiritually warped for the rest of their lives, being subjected to such horrors in fragile childhood.

We ask it, O God.

We pray that adults who are forcing young people into such depravation will recognize that they are destroying not only the lives of children, but their country's future, for a nation of psychically wounded people is not a healthy nation.

We ask it, O God.

We pray that the scourge of land mines will abate, and that those who have been wounded and disabled by them will find the strength to go on.

We ask it, O God.

We pray that leaders of our own nation will declare the United States' unequovical opposition to the use of landmines.

We ask it, O God.

We pray for the thousands and thousands of displaced children in Africa and throughout the world. Be with them and help them in these terrible times of trial.

We ask it, O God.

Although we live on the other side of the world, give us the will, the vision, the diligence, and the discipline to do what we can to make a difference in the lives of these children. Be with us and guide us as we seek to live our lives as you would wish.

We ask it, O God, in the name of your son. Amen.

Preparation for Session 3
Reading: Chapter 4, *Children of Africa.*
Ask for a volunteer to present as a closing devotion after Session 3, the biblical reflection by Elizabeth S. Tapia, printed at the end of the session. This could be done either as straight reading from the text or as some sort of adaptation: perhaps the volunteer might be Ms. Tapia, since the reflection draws on her personal experience.

Session 3: *The Shattered Lives of Forgotten Children*

Brief Opening Worship

Again, use the Bible passage and prayer, if you wish, as well as hymn suggestions in the appendix.

The Spirit of the Lord is upon me, because he has anointed me to bring good news to the poor. He has sent me to proclaim release to the captives and recovery of sight to the blind, to let the oppressed go free, to proclaim the year of the Lord's favor. (Luke 4 :18, 19)

Dear God, be with us today as we continue to examine the lives of your children—those children in Africa who are suffering poverty, hunger, loneliness, and abuse. As we learn about their plight, grant us compassion. But grant us also the discipline, the persistence, the toughness, and the resilience we need so that our compassion may bear fruit in the form of help—even from our distant and comfortable perch—to reduce some of these terrible and seemingly hopeless situations. We ask it in the name of your son, Jesus Christ. Amen.

Objectives

- To learn more about the lives of Africa's street children
- To learn more about the lives of children sold into slavery
- To learn more about the reality of child labor, the various kinds of child labor, and the threats that face children who are doing such work
- To learn more about the underlying reasons for these situations, and what is being done by African nations to resolve them

Introduction to Session 3

The material in this session is in many ways heartbreaking. However, it gets to the nub of the hopeless and despairing reality of many African children. As leader, you will introduce your group to the lives of these children after the wars are over; after the death or loss of parents; after removal from country to city. In huge numbers of cases, the former child soldiers, the former child prostitutes, the orphans, the children of desperately poor parents end up on the streets of large African cities—usually hungry, often sick, and with no futures. As you and the group think about and discuss how such situations develop, ask yourselves what the affected nations must do to improve them, and what other nations—and the global community—can do to help.

Vignette

> There's a street in one of the nicer parts of Luanda where children live packed into the storm drains underneath the road. People passing by see young heads peering out of the gutters. They are small children who were separated from their families during the war, or whose parents are too poor to support them. They sleep in the drains because it is safer than sleeping in the streets.
> ——— BBC *Focus on Africa* Magazine, July/September 1998, p. 51 [Onwu, chapter 4]

A. Street Children

Analysis

Often the end of wars, writes Onwu, but also displacement from rural areas to the city, means life on the streets for a variety of children: former child soldiers with no home to return to; young girls formerly held by military groups who now turn to prostitution; orphans and refugee children looking for food; whole families who were driven from their homes during the fighting; those who cannot return home because of land mines, polluted water, and other environmental factors.

For Discussion
- Where and how, within a city, do you think these children live? Do they have any kind of support system?
- What do they do to support themselves? Do any of them have families? What do the families do?
- What are the tragic consequences in the development of these children, who have lost all opportunity for a safe, secure upbringing?
- What are the prospects for a nation that has large numbers of such children, reared on the streets, used to lying and stealing for mere survival, growing up into an untrained, uneducated adulthood devoid of real prospects?
- What sort of an impact is the homeless situation in our own country having on our society? How can it be addressed?

Exercise

Ask group participants each to try visualizing one specific African young person who lives on the streets. Ask them to imagine how that person lives—either with parents, other children, or alone—and what he/she does to survive. Try to imagine the personality, age, appearance, and gender of that person. Then distribute writing materials and ask group participants to write a personal, chatty, supportive, friendly letter to that person, asking how he/she is doing, what the group member is doing, etc. Toward the end of session ask for volunteers to read their letters to the group.

Exercise

Read in Onwu, chapter 4, about South African female and male prostitutes, and their answers when interrogated about their lives. Set up a situation, either as a whole group or several smaller groups, in which an interrogator asks questions, such as those in the survey, of group members who play the role of the youth being questioned. Let group members ask themselves about the profound unfairness of blaming such young people for behavior which is for them the most undesirable and shameful, but possibly the only, form of survival.

B. Slavery

Analysis

We Americans almost define the word "slavery" by our own past history and the scars that continue to have a profound effect on our society. But slavery continues. According to UNICEF estimates, writes Onwu, more than 1 million women and children throughout the world are sold each year, and the slave trade is big business in the interior of Sudan.

Vignette (Read about Deng in Onwu, chapter 4.)

For Discussion

- Discuss the situation in Sudan, where a Swiss-based human-rights organization has paid Arab traders large sums to recover members of the Dinka tribe who had been sold into slavery. Why has the Swiss organization been criticized for its actions? Do you agree? Why? Why not?
- In practical terms, how are such abductions into slavery carried out? Why would parents permit their children to become slaves?

C. Child Labor

Vignette

Asabe Mohammed, a 14-year-old food hawker from the village of Soro in Nigeria, had been on the street selling food cooked by her mother throughout her primary school years. 'I think I was not that big when I started hawking food,' she commented, pointing to a seven-year-old girl. But Asabe had a second chance, attending the Soro Girl-Child Education Center, established in May 1993 as part of an initiative by UNICEF and the Nigerian Government."

────── *The State of the World's Children, 1999*, UNICEF [Onwu, chapter 4]

(Read about young people hawking goods on the street, Onwu, chapter 4.)

Vignette

In Nigeria, writes Onwu, this trade represents a boycott by a specific tribal group, the Ibo, against an educational system that has totally failed its young people. Interestingly, young people work for importers of huge quantities of goods, who hire the teens as sales persons. Often the parents do not object because the work pays good wages.

Chima Ezonyejiaku is one of these boys. His father is a retired head teacher and his mother still teaches in a village school, yet Chima has abandoned his studies to apprentice himself to a wealthy trader in the town of Onitsha. Like most of his friends, he feels that school is a waste of time and wants to begin the process of making money.

────── *The State of the World's Children 1999*, UNICEF [Onwu, chapter 4]

Exercise

This is a skit in which volunteers will be the parents of children who are attending school (and therefore not earning money), and the parents of children like Chima in the vignette, who have become salespersons for well-to-do traders. There might be poor parents, but also some that are more comfortably off. Let them discuss the pros and cons of schooling for their children. Although this is not specifically aimed at girls' issues, it would be good if some of them had daughters, to see how they feel about schooling them. (If volunteers have prepared this skit in advance, ask them to present it to the group.) Ask the whole group to discuss the presentation when it's over.

As is true in most societies, a certain amount of work for children in positive situations is a good thing, and this is also a cultural and societal norm in much of Africa. "No doubt," says UNICEF in its 1997 report on the state of the world's children, "some of the work promotes or enhances their development, without interfering with schooling, recreation and rest, however, much of it is palpably destructive with poor children facing such hazards because they are exploited." [Onwu, chapter 4]

Discussion

- What are some of the numerous reasons that children in Africa work? Do most of them have a choice? Are we talking only about children of extremely poor, uneducated parents?
- What is the connection between children at work and a society with no welfare or other social safety net?

Vignette

Listen to Isaac Nkundabantu of Rwanda as he reports on the 1994 Rwandan genocide, and reflect on what it means in the lives (and deaths) of untold numbers of Rwandan children: "About one million people were killed, some say in just three months. In addition to death and injury, human and material resources were lost, impacting the economy. The environment was spoiled, as bodies were thrown into rivers and trees were cut down everywhere. The violence created psychological trauma and had a major impact on health conditions. To my knowledge, no relief work was done during the genocide. Relief work came in at the end."

——— Weaver, "Disaster Management Training in Africa,"
New World Outlook, Jan/Feb 1999, p. 35.

Exercise

Ask a volunteer to introduce Isaac Nkundabantu of the above vignette to the group, and ask another volunteer to "be" Mr. Nkundabantu and speak his words, as reproduced above. Then let there be a discussion, as people ask him—and themselves—probing questions about the whole Rwanda disaster: What were some of the reasons for the terrible violence? Why were bodies thrown into rivers and trees cut down? Why do you think other nations in the world (including our own) looked on from afar and did little or nothing? How does this compare with U.S. concern for Kosovo and Israel, for example? Is it enough to say, "Rwanda is not important to

America"? (For further information about Rwanda, see Elizabeth Ferris's *Uprooted! Refugees and Forced Migrants*, the Friendship Press study book for 1998.)

What We Can Do

By now, group members have familiarized themselves with the listings in chapter 7 and Session 5. If they wish, this might be a good time to discuss the possibilities for specific participation, action, or giving, to some of the projects listed. Perhaps a volunteer could do further research before the next session about specific UMC programs or other ways of helping that are of interest to group participants.

Exercise: Songs and Play of Africa's Children

Perhaps you will want to repeat one of the songs used before. Or you may wish to choose a new one. Or a game. Think about the street children you have discussed. Games, especially, may be the one playful activity in which they can indulge—perhaps stolen moments away from their tasks, whatever they may be. As for singing and dancing—these have always been healers of the soul, available to everyone.

Biblical Reflection: So No One Lives in Pain

The following Bible study was presented at Assembly '98 by Elizabeth S. Tapia, ordained Methodist elder and professor of theology at Union Theological Seminary in the Philippines. Ms. Tapia speaks out of the experience of an impoverished childhood in a non-African developing country, in ways that speak to all people. It is a reminder to us, as we learn about impoverished and exploited children in Africa that, although Africa may be in particularly difficult straits at this time, poverty is not limited to that continent. Ms. Tapia presented the following Bible study.

"The Spirit of the Lord is upon me, because God has anointed me to bring good news to the poor. God has sent me to proclaim release to the captives and recovery of sight to the blind, to let the oppressed go free, to proclaim the year of the Lord's favor." Luke 4: 18, 19

Bible-study leader Elizabeth S. Tapia began by asking Assembly participants to pray with hands and eyes open. Looking to Luke, Habakkuk and Isaiah, she spoke of a vision where no one lives in pain:

"Hear the lamentations of a street child," she said. "I am a girl . . . a homeless child, living on the streets of Manila [or Brazzaville or Nairobi or Johannesburg or Kigali]. While other children have homes and gardens, the garbage heap is my garden, the dirty street my home. God, why? Don't tell me why."

Ms. Tapia . . . told her audience she grew up in poverty. "My parents could hardly support us 11 children," she said. "Our eldest sister died at age three. In the Philippines, 80 percent of the 70 million population live below the poverty line."

"What is the good news to the poor?" Ms. Tapia asked, then said, "People become poor when they are brokenhearted and without hope. They become poor when they are dispossessed and discriminated against. People die when the land is devastated. Therefore, the poor need to hear the good news." "Sharing the good news means sharing Jesus' vision for the world," she said.

"Jesus' vision-mission is liberation for all," Ms. Tapia said. "It is a vision of healing and wholeness, of peace and justice, of hope and joy. Jesus' vision is total liberation for all."

Ms. Tapia explained that in the Gospel of Luke, the *poor* refers primarily to the materially poor. She quoted Luke 6:20: "The poor are those who have no sustenance, no social status and power," she said. "The majority of them are women, widows, orphaned children, the sick and those unable to work."

She asked Assembly participants to envision new heavens on earth. She asked they not give up but keep working and praying until justice prevails. "Make the vision plain, so no one lives in pain" Ms. Tapia implored. "We need to walk in the path of harmlessness. . . ."

She said of the women of her country: "These women know how to make faith visible. They teach me that in the midst of hunger or drought or flood, don't give up. In the midst of calamity and isolation, cling to hope. In the midst of struggle, celebrate life."

— Hunter, A. Victoria *Response*, October 1998, p. 7.

Closing Prayer

Preparation for Session 4
Reading: Chapter 5, *Children of Africa*
Ask for a volunteer (or two volunteers) to prepare a closing litany based on the material to be discussed. Remind them to make photocopies of the litany for group members.

Session 4: Education, the Healer; Decisions of Nations—their Impact on Children

Brief Opening Worship

The Bible passages and prayer below may be used, as well as hymns from the United Methodist Hymnal and a selection of African hymns in the Appendices. Or you may wish to open with prayer and use the litany at the end of this session as part of a brief closing worship service.

My people are destroyed for lack of knowledge. (Hosea 4:6)

On either side of the river is the tree of life with its twelve kinds of fruit, producing its fruit each month; and the leaves of the tree are for the healing of the nations. (Rev. 22:2)

Dear God, Help us learn what we can do to improve the lives and futures of so many African children. Help us remember that we are all a part of your family—and that it behooves us to care for one another. We ask it in the name of your son, Jesus Christ, who loved the poor, the destitute, the stricken—and especially the children.

Objectives
- To learn about the breakdown in children's education throughout Africa, and the reasons for it
- To learn how/why political and economic decisions at the highest levels impinge on lives—including those of children—at the very lowest levels.

A. Education, the Healer

Analysis

As the 21st century makes its entrance, nearly a billion people will still not be able to read and write: functional illiterates, victims of societies where they have not had access to basic education, or where they have been in substandard schools where little learning takes place, or where they have been denied schooling because they were girls. According to UNICEF's *State of the World's Children 1999*, "[Education] is . . . the single most vital element in combating poverty, empowering women, safeguarding children from exploitative and hazardous labor and sexual exploitation. It is critical in promoting human rights and democracy, protecting the environment, and controlling population growth."

Vignette

The pupils of Morris Isaacson high school in Soweto once led an uprising against apartheid education. At morning assembly, one day in 1976, they shocked their teachers by loudly singing "Nkosi Sikelel'i Afrika," (God Bless Africa), an African hymn that is now the South African national anthem. They then marched out to the streets to join other students in the protest, bloodily suppressed, that was to set the tone for nearly two decades of struggle.

In those days, Morris Isaacson was a hotbed not only of radicalism but of academic excellence. The school produced revolutionaries, doctors and South Africa's only black nuclear physicist. Today, it is a mess. Pupils wander around aimlessly when they should be at lessons. Classroom doors are barred; coils of razor wire defend the playground. Three-quarters of Morris Isaacson students fail to graduate; only 2% make it to university. And this is one of the most popular schools in Soweto.

The problem is not lack of money. South Africa spends more on education than most countries of similar wealth. The buildings at Morris Isaacson are pleasant. But two things prevent most black South Africans from fulfilling their academic potential: unruliness in the classroom and incompetence at the education ministry.

The 1976 uprising was sparked by the government's insistence that black children should learn Afrikaans, the hated language of the oppressors. Soon, the protests broadened their scope. Pupils boycotted classes to demand an end to white rule itself. The slogan was "liberation before education." Unfortunately, the rowdiness outlived liberation.

"We are trying to revive the culture of learning," says Elias Mashile, the head of Morris Isaacson, "but it takes time."

———*The Economist*, May 15, 1999, p. 46.

For Discussion:

- Ask the group to examine the Morris Isaacson vignette. Why do you think there has been such a serious breakdown? How does the colonial legacy—in this case, South Africa's apartheid legacy—play into this?
- What does Onwu say about teachers' pay?
- Are there still remnants of colonial systems of education? Are they favored, or not? Why? How do parents respond to the situation?
- Can we draw comparisons with our own history of slavery and all-too-recent apartheid policies, and the impact they have had/still have on students?

Exercise

Ask the group to divide into two groups to hold a debate about the future of education in Africa. Ask them to try thinking of themselves as African parents, concerned about the future of their children. In some ways, the debate may raise the same kinds of emotional responses as discussions in the United States about public education vs. vouchers: Team 1: African school systems must think about developing teaching curricula that speak to local situations; Team 2: African school systems should copy the educational systems of the ex-colonial powers which have produced some of the most effective African leaders. Defend/argue these positions.

Exercise

Make a sign: "Welcome to the 23rd Reunion of Morris Isaacson High School Class of 1977." Ask for volunteers to represent graduates: several teachers, a lawyer, a doctor, several farmers (remember that farmers in Africa are usually women), etc. Then ask a volunteer to read the Morris Isaacson Highschool vignette, above. After the volunteer has finished, let the role play begin with the actors' discussion of the fateful day in 1976, discussed in the vignette. Then let them compare the condition of current education as compared with the excellent education they got over two decades ago. They can discuss reasons, solutions, etc.

Another interesting way of handling vignettes might be the following: Ask a volunteer to read the vignette aloud to the group, and have others act out the words in pantomime. For example, at the very beginning, when the words "the pupils" are read in line one, three people suddenly stand and start singing (silently!), and then march to the other side of the room. In the second paragraph, when the words "revolutionaries, doctors, and South Africa's only black nuclear physicist" are read, persons get up, gesticulating as they "speak" for change, taking temperatures or examining "patients", etc. (again, all in pantomime). When the volunteer reads "Today it is a mess. Pupils wander around aimlessly . . ." let some "pupils" do just that. When "Three-quarters of Morris Isaacson school students fail to graduate" is read, all of the actors might slump in disinterest or despair. Ask the group to work out its own ideas. Then, the appropriate actors in the pantomime can take part in the "Morris Isaacson Reunion" and probe the topic even further.

2. Education for Girls
Analysis (Read in Onwu, chapter 2, about education for girls vs. boys)

Exercises
- Create "Peril of Being a Girl" cards. Let each person in the group write a key difficulty affecting education for girls. Divide into small groups, and give each group several of the cards. Ask group members to a) discuss the situation stated on the card in an African context; b) draw parallels from U.S. or other country contexts; c) draft a potential solution to easing or erasing the peril.
- Discuss the work of the Forum for African Women Educationalists (FAWE) or the African Girls' Education Initiative. How can we support them?

3. Education for Disabled Children
(Read Onwu's vignette about education for disabled children, chapter 2.)

Exercise
Ask someone in the group to read the vignette in Onwu's book. Discuss with group. Then ask another person to read the paragraph about the Uhuru Mchanganyiko school. Discuss.

For Discussion
We dare not be smug. Today, since their release from large institutions, mentally disabled persons make up a large percentage of America's homeless population, especially in large urban centers. What do group members think about the way the U.S. is handling these challenges? How do group members

evaluate what is happening in many African countries? And how, do they think, can situations such as the one at the Nigerian school for the blind be overcome in a society that regards physical and mental affliction with great suspicion?

B. Decisions of Nations—Their Impact on Children

We know that new economic and political patterns are sweeping our globalizing post-cold war world in ways that we do not yet fully comprehend. In order to understand this new world, we need to know something about the International Monetary Fund, the World Bank, and the concept of structural adjustment. And we need to understand why they have such a direct effect on a nation's individuals— usually its poorest and its children.

A. Political and Economic Realities

Analysis

It is not easy to understand why so many efforts to improve the conditions of poor nations through various kinds of financial assistance have not worked. Many experts feel that the approach of the International Monetary Fund has been disastrous—leaving the poor of many developing countries more impoverished than ever. But there are also those who believe that other forms of external aid have not achieved self-sustaining economic growth nor prevented the collapse of poor societies over the past decades.

> Few programs have consumed as many resources with as few positive results as foreign aid. . . . Yet the recipients of that largess, by and large, have failed to grow economically and develop democratically. In many cases it has underwritten brutal dictators as they have pillaged their peoples; in other instances, Western financial flows have subsidized the creation of disastrously inefficient state-led development programs. . . . have backed regimes that were both corrupt and collectivist. . . . Not only was the money used poorly, it often buttressed the very governments that were most responsible for the ensuing disasters. . . .most aid benefitted local political elites.

> Many governments simply are not interested in policy reform. Some of them want their countries to develop but are unwilling to pay the political price for adopting policies necessary to do so. Others treat ideological objectives as paramount. Still others are mot interest-

ed in staying in power. By masking the pain of economic failure, development assistance allows borrowers to delay reforms, worsening the underlying problem.

———— Bandow, Doug. "Foreign Aid Does Not Prevent Social Breakdown,"

USA Today, March 1998.

For Discussion

- Define structural adjustment and explain its effect on citizens of a country that is subjected to it. Why do so many experts feel that it has a negative effect on the population of a receiver country? Are there statistics that bear this out?
- Do you understand why many of those responsible for African development do not believe that structural adjustment will work?
- Our history books make clear that the United States did not achieve overnight its current state of freedom and justice How can we expect African nations, with their various histories of colonialism and oppression, to develop in one or two generations the tools, know-how, and discipline required for a democratic form of government? What does the group think? Are there parallels?
- Onwu in her introduction writes, "The children are the first to succumb to wars, famine, diseases, natural disasters and the like. They are also the first to be victimized by the physical and moral decadence of their societies." Do you agree? Give examples in the text. Is this also true in the United States? If so, give examples.

> **Exercise** *(Read about Jubilee 2000 in Onwu, chapter 5.)*
>
> Many in America think that the best way the West can help Africa is to forgive billions of dollars in loans that the countries owe to the United States. Church World Service of the National Council of Churches, as part of its Jubilee 2000, endorses a worldwide movement to cancel the crushing international debt of impoverished countries by the new millennium. Divide the group in half and engage in the following debate, pro and con: Debt forgiveness, as proposed by certain groups as part of their Jubilee 2000 celebration would be a good and beneficial thing for debtor nations.
>
> **Exercise**
>
> Divide the group (or not, if it is small) so that there are no more than four or five people in one small grouping. Let each small group think of itself as the top policy-making body of an African country. Based on what the whole group has learned, let the small groups try to work out policy that would best serve the whole country. Let them try to figure out what roadblocks

they would encounter (particularly greed and corruption, but also poor infrastructure, lack of modern communications systems, etc.) for putting into place better hospitals, for example, or schools or, even, more responsive and responsible government. Ask the small groups to come together at the end, and leave some time for each to make its report.

Positive Trends

Analysis *(Read quote about positive signs in Africa,* Time *magazine article, Onwu, chapter 5.)*

For Discussion.
- What are some of the positive signs in African development?
- Why is it, even though Africa is an extremely rich continent with a population full of high potential, that most of its people are so desperately poor?
- How has current leadership changed during recent years? How have current African leaders learned from past failures?

B. Rights of Children

1. The Convention on the Rights of the Child

"The idea that children have special needs has given way to the conviction that children have rights, the same full spectrum of rights as adults: civil and political, social, cultural and economic."

— *The State of the World's Children* 1997, UNICEF, Oxford University Press, United Kingdom.

After the adoption of the above statement by the UN General Assembly on September 2, 1990, it was entered into international law as the Convention on the Rights of the Child (CRC). It has since been ratified by nearly all countries on the African continent.

2. African Children Speak Up for Their Rights

(Read piece about Sinton High in Onwu, chapter 5.)

For Discussion
- Ask group participants to think about the implications of the Convention on the Rights of the Child for children throughout the world. Do you believe that it can make a difference, or is it no more

than a well-meaning effort that has little actual effect on the lives of actual children?
- According to Onwu, the world is making a revolutionary shift in approach toward children as the world strives toward peace, equality, and justice for all. Do you agree? Why? Why not?
- What do you think the statement by the Sinton High School students says about African youth? Do you sense that there is a new generation preparing itself for leadership?

Exercise

Ask the group to think itself back to high school days—let's say a student council meeting. Only this time, it's at Sinton High in West Cape, South Africa, and the group is preparing to draft the statement just read. Ask the group to engage in the sort of discussion that might lead to the statement. On a chalkboard or newsprint, let one person write down points that should be included in the statement. At the end, have someone in the group read the finished statement to general applause for a job well done.

Exercise

Divide into small groups. Discuss actual instances here at home and in Africa, in which the Convention on the Rights of the Child, if it were really taken seriously, could make a significant difference in the treatment of children. Write them down, or be prepared to share your findings with the whole group. Discuss. Do you think that here in the United States, over the past fifty years, there have been positive/negative changes in the way we treat our children?

What *We* Can Do

Do group members have ideas or suggestions? The group may wish to make some concrete plans for action.

Exercise

Songs and Play of Africa's Children

Just a reminder if you wish to use some of the songs and games in the appendix. And remember, if there's to be an African evening, plans should be well advanced by now!

Litany

We pray for those in positions of political power throughout the world. Guide them to make decisions that do not ignore the poorest and most fragile of their own societies and of those countries over whose fate they have influence and power.

Be with them, O God, in their deliberations.
We pray for those leaders, in both private and public positions, who are shaping the economies of the world. Help them and guide them to make decisions that do more than enrich the few at the expense of the many.

Be with them, O God, and grant them compassion and wisdom.
We pray for leaders in Africa. Give them the courage and the strength to make decisions that will improve the lives of all, including the poorest and most vulnerable.

Be with them, O God, as they struggle to lead their nation-states.
We pray for those many who are governed in ways that make their lives difficult and in many cases intolerable.

Give them the strength, O God, to cope.
We pray for the many parents caught in the vise of war, hunger, destruction, and disease, without the power to make changes for themselves and their children.

Give them strength and resilience, O God, until their lives improve.
We pray for the many children in Africa whose lives at this moment seem hopeless.

Give them a future, O God, filled with good things.
We pray for those young people in Africa whose lives are good and who are being educated.

Be with them, O God, that they may provide stability and wise leadership in the future.
We pray for ourselves, O God, that we may not grow oblivious to those in the world that need our help. Give us the discipline and the commitment to respond. We ask it all in the name of your son, Jesus Christ. Amen.

Preparation for Session 5

Reading: Chapters 6 and 7, *Children of Africa*

Reserve some time so that group members who kept a journal during this study may read extracts to the group: those things that particularly moved, angered, encouraged, or discouraged them, and their ideas about how what they have learned may be applied after the study is over.

Ask for volunteers to prepare a closing worship at the end of Session 5. Let the volunteers choose how they want to do it: as a litany, responsive prayers, scripture readings—whatever seems most effective for summing up the entire study. An African hymn that can be used as a litany is found at the end of Session 5.

5: The Church in Africa—Source of Caring, Courage, and Hope

Brief Opening Worship

The volunteers who were asked to prepare worship for this session may want to do it either as opening or closing worship. If they choose to do it at the end, summing up the whole study, they may wish to open with only a brief prayer. Note, at the end of this session, the African hymn structured as a litany.

When the apostle Paul sought help among the congregations for people in Jerusalem who were living in poverty, he noted the importance of mutual responsibility: "It is a question of a fair balance between your present abundance and their need." (2 Cor. 8:13b-14a)

Suppose a brother or a sister is in rags with not enough food for the day, and one of you says, 'Good luck to you, keep yourselves warm, and have plenty to eat; but does nothing to supply their bodily needs, what is the good of that? So with faith; if it does not lead to action, it is in itself a lifeless thing." (James 2:15-17)

We thank you, O God, for these past weeks of study. During this, our last session, as we study the work of the church and other groups throughout Africa—in particular, as they address the needs of children—be with us as we ponder our own role in these massive efforts. Help us be steadfast in our concern for Africa's people and its children, even though this formal study is at an end, that we may continue to follow the news, find information through our church press, and involve ourselves in lightening the burden currently borne by millions of children in Africa. Be with them and help them, O God, in their time of need. And be with us, as well, as we seek to do your will. Amen

Objectives

- To look briefly at the early and colonial history of the African Church, to recognize its amazing vitality and growth in our own day, and to learn something about its current work with dispossessed young Africans
- To learn what The United Methodist Church is doing in modern Africa—particularly as it affects the theme of our study
- To learn what we can do—even from far away—as individuals, as church people, as citizens of a rapidly developing global village

Introduction to Session 5

In this session you and the group will examine the African church—its earliest beginnings, its colonial history, and its enormous vitality and growth in our own day. Having established that context, we return to our theme and focus on ways in which the African church is working with physically and spiritually needy young people. The session continues with a look at the ongoing work in Africa of the Western church, particularly The United Methodist Church. Then the group will have the opportunity to explore what secular groups, African and others, small and large, are doing to address the problems of Africa's violated children. Finally, as we reach the end of our study, we ask ourselves the all-important question: What can we do, as members of the global village?

A. The African Church *(Read the excerpts from speeches of Archbishop Desmond Tutu and Jose Chipenda at the General Assembly of the All-African Council of Churches: Onwu, chapter 6.)*

For Discussion

The concept of the "global village" originated in Africa. What does it mean? How can it work? How can we all participate?

B. The Western Church in Africa

Analysis (Read section about the Western Church in Africa, Onwu, chapter 6.)

For Discussion

- Discuss the earliest history of Christianity in Africa.
- What did Jomo Kenyatta mean? If you were an African, looking back on colonial history, would you agree? Do you, as a Westerner, agree?
- Why does Onwu note that the struggle against imperialism owes much to the Christian impact upon Africa? Do you agree/disagree? Why?
- How is it important that so many of Africa's current leaders have been products of western Christian missionary education? Ask someone to research some of these leaders (Nelson Mandela is, of course, the best-known) and report to the group.

C. The United Methodist Church in Africa Today

UMCOR

UMCOR has created a new section, now referred to as the NGO unit. NGO is a common term in relief-agency circles, standing for "nongovernmental organization." Our NGO is located in Arlington, Virginia, among a great many other similar organizations, or NGOs. Each offers to assist governments, government departments, the United Nations, the European Union, and a host of large ecumenical organizations and philanthropic foundations in applying aid monies to massive social problems. These large donors want to send funds to countries in desperate struggles, but they need the likes of us—with our experience and solid reputation for truly providing help—to do it well.

Having an NGO arm is a great opportunity. In the last three years, we have used an average of $1.8 million per year that we received from United Methodist members to facilitate an average of $25 million per year that we receive from institutions which want to build on United Methodists' original generosity in relief and basic development. We have so far built on this generosity in Bosnia, Armenia, Azerbaijan, Georgia, Liberia, Rwanda, and Haiti. In such places as these, no "reed bent by the wind" will do.

——— Dirdak, Paul. *New World Outlook*, Jan/Feb 1999, p. 6.

Emergency Response Training in Africa

The United Methodist Committee on Relief (UMCOR) and the Geneva-based Action by Churches Together (ACT), an ecumenical relief organization, have formed a partnership with Africa University to present training sessions on emergency response and management in Africa. Representatives from countries throughout Africa have been sent to Mutare, Zimbabwe, for the first 6-week training session, June 22-July 31. Increasing Africa's ability to prepare for and manage emergencies is crucial for UMCOR and ACT, said Lloyd Rollins, an executive in UMCOR's Office of Emergency Services. "UMCOR and ACT want Africans to determine what the program needs to be and how it will be implemented," he said, "rather than having it imposed by outsiders who supply the funding."

——— "Mission Memo," *New World Outlook*, July/August 1998, p. 42.

Vignette

"Amy Peel of Orlando, Florida, has experienced the global village concept as a UMC mission intern in Johannesburg, South Africa. She worked primarily with pre-school children in a program called FLOC (For Love of Children). This program is for poor children in Johannesburg, and is funded partially by the Women's Division of the General Board of Global Ministries, The United Methodist Church. Excerpt from Ms. Peel's letter to the General Board: "The children are the delight of my days and a symbol of hope that this country will be able to start again. My major responsibilities include chapel time for the children, weekly Bible stories, staff devotions, and individual work with children and staff. . . . I am also helping to integrate an anti-bias/peace education curriculum into the classroom. This has been incredibly exciting and inspiring! The teachers are a close-knit community of women with whom I do a lot of interacting. . . . I feel truly blessed to be welcomed into their lives." [Onwu, chapter 7]

Bishops' Appeal and Campaign Fund for Africa

Their resilience is amazing. Across the continent of Africa, despite the many strides in commerce, education and community development, the scars of civil war, colonial rape-and-pillage, corrupt government, poverty and hunger mar the land.

Still, the children's faces shine with hope, with promise, with goodness, with the faith that God has great plans for the sons and daughters of what is arguably still the most misunderstood continent in the modern world.

It is this hope, seen through the eyes of children, that has touched the bishops of The United Methodist church—those born in Africa and those from other nations.

And it is with that hope that the bishops now challenge the entire denomination to put dollars, cents, prayers and human resources to work to make a difference in the future of African children, their families and their communities.

——— from "For Our Children: A Living Hope (Bishops' Appeal [on GBGM website])

The Bishops' Appeal and Campaign fund is a five-year effort to raise extra gifts for extraordinary times. It aims to provide relief and reconciliation to thousands of children and families who have suffered and lost so much from war across the continent; rebuild United Methodist churches and restore ministries, with special attention to the physical, social, and spiritual wellbeing of children. Programs fall under four categories: children's health; children's education; children of war; and social, emotional, and spiritual nurture of children.

Bishops' Initiative on Children and Poverty

The Bishops' Initiative on Children and Poverty is an effort to confront the social, economic, political, moral, and spiritual concerns that cast a growing number of people, especially children, into poverty. "In Gisenyi, Rwanda, there are now forty children in a small community. They have no parents, and those who are lucky are cared for by an extended family. These children are receiving housing and education partly through the gifts of other children in Onondoga Hill United Methodist Church near Syracuse, NY. Pastor Jupa, wanting more for these children, and with the help of local children, began to build a house and educate

———— Bishop Forest C. Stith, "Children Helping Children in Rwanda"

Other Initiatives

Operation Classroom: A project of the Indiana Conference that offers support for UMC schools in Sierra Leone. To contact, please write to Operation Classroom, The United Methodist Church, 207 West Jackson Street., P.O. Box 277, Colfax, IN.

Volunteers in Mission: United Methodist conferences or churches in the United States can form a VIM team to go to a destination in Africa for a limited period in order to help with specific, focused projects: repair or construction of buildings, and a large range of other services. Arrangements for such a trip can be made through Volunteers in Mission, General Board of Global Ministries, New York, NY.

Africa University: Located in Mutare, Zimbabwe, Africa University is the first institution of higher education established by The United Methodist Church on the African continent for the purpose of educating students from countries throughout the continent. For further information about how you can help Africa University and its students, contact James Salley, Board of Higher Education, Nashville, TN.

All-Africa Women's Desk: This is part of the All-Africa Conference of Churches. For information about projects sponsored by this desk, please contact Battu Jawambai, Women's Desk, All-Africa Conference of Churches, Nairobi, Kenya.

Women's, children's, and youth desks of African annual conferences, or other Methodist national church offices are other excellent sources for information about what support you can lend.

Exercise

Let the group think of itself as a local church mission work area. It is charged with the responsibility of deciding local church mission giving: how to allocate the congregation's $3,000 set aside for mission. This is a big responsibility, requiring considerable information about possible uses, UMC programs, possible needs that haven't yet been properly considered, etc. Let the group, with use of the chalk board or newsprint, work out and write up a carefully considered use of mission funds for children of Africa.

What We Can Do

- Set aside a significant portion of this final session to discuss—perhaps in small groups, perhaps as a whole group—the many possibilities (just hinted at above) for engagement by individuals in the UMC's work throughout Africa. What are these possibilities? What individual/group efforts could be developed? How and where would one begin? What programs have been initiated by the Women's Division of the General Board of Global Ministries?
- Write a Mission Minute—to be shared aloud in the group and to be given in church about the joys and concerns of children in Africa.

Closing Litany (prepared by volunteers) or
African Hymn To Be Used as a Litany

Leader: Let the people know: *Group:* messengers are present here.
Leader: Let the people know: *Group:* messengers are present here.
Leader: Let the people know: *Group:* messengers are present here.
All: For the strength to witness we give thanks, O God.
Leader: Tell to all around,   *Group:* "Witnesses are present here."
Leader: Tell to all around,   *Group:* "Witnesses are present here."
Leader: Tell to all around,   *Group:* "Witnesses are present here."
All: For the strength to witness we give thanks, O God.

114

Leader: Give strength to our hearts, *Group:* faithful we would always be . . .

Leader: Give strength to our hearts, *Group:* faithful we would always be . . .

Leader: Give strength to our hearts, *Group:* faithful we would always be . . .

All: For the strength to witness we give thanks, O God.

Leader: Alleluia, sing,   *Group:* God is with us here and now . . .

Leader: Alleluia, sing,   *Group:* God is with us here and now . . .

Leader: Alleluia, sing,   *Group:* God is with us here and now . . .

All: For the strength to witness we give thanks, O God.

—— Shukuru Alla (Let the People Know) Words and music, trad. South-Sudan, Africa; English, S T Kimbrough, Jr., *Global Praise I*, No. 56, General Board of Global Ministries, 1996

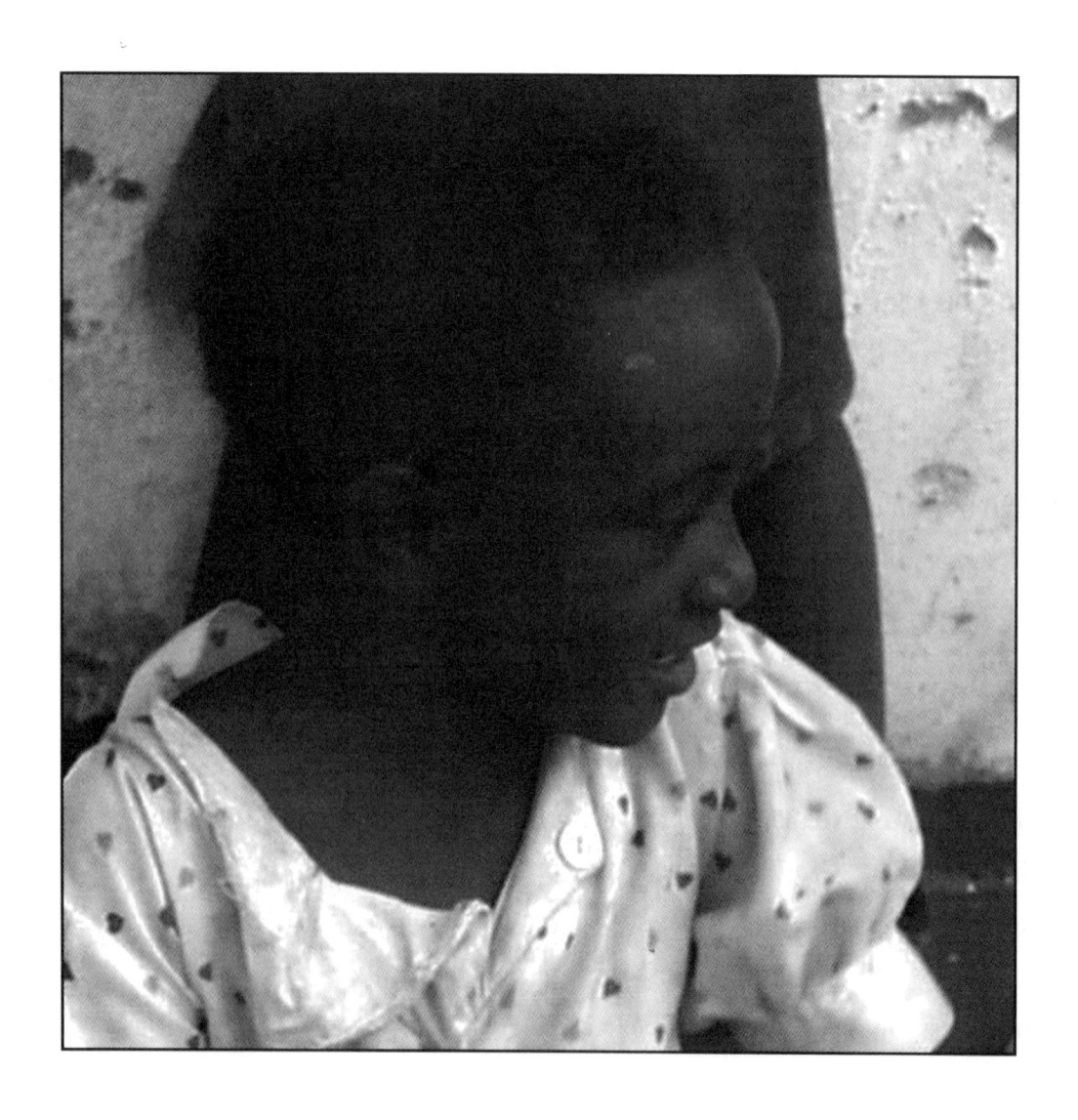

Appendix 1

African Quiz

1. What are three things that come immediately to mind when you think of Africa?

2. Name the largest, second-largest, and smallest continents on Earth.

3. Can you name any African rivers and their approximate location?

4. Africa has a spectacular array of natural resources, many of which have hardly been touched. Do you know for what exports Africa is known today?

5. Can you name some of the former colonial powers and the current names of the countries they colonized?

6. What were the decades during which most of the former African colonies were granted independence? Can you name some of them?

7. Did you know that Africa has the longest human history of any continent? Do you know far back indications of human life have been traced?

8. It is estimated that there are more than _____ spoken languages in Africa.

9. Which country in Africa has the earliest history of Christianity?

10. What are the African countries in which the United Methodist Church works? What are some of the things the UMC does in those countries?

11. Do you know the names and locations of the annual conferences of the Methodist church in Africa?

Answers/Comments

[1] Africa is a continent of such astonishing variety, that it is almost impossible to generalize. As the West finally begins thinking of it as more than one entity, usually dismissed as the "Dark Continent," we are developing a far more sophisticated understanding of Africa than ever before. One (rather superficial) way of becoming aware of Africa's variety is a glance at a travel guide like *Lonely Planet*. If it does nothing else, such a brief look at Africa--nation by nation-- suggests the continent's multitude of distinctive physical attributes, climates, wild life, cultures, and peoples.

[2] Largest: *Asia; second-largest*: Africa; smallest: Australia.

[3] Nile (the world's longest river; Congo; Niger, Limpopo, Senegal. [Look them up on a geographical map of Africa. Check your encyclopedia.]

[4] Peanuts, cocoa, rare and precious minerals (including most of the world's diamonds). In spite of the general perception of Africa, based on the extreme poverty of much of its population, it is by no means a poor continent. Despite colonial plunder, Africa continues to have a huge and diverse array of natural resources, from minerals and oil to spectacular scenery and wildlife.

[5] Ghana, Kenya, Nigeria, Sierra Leone, Tanzania, Zimbabwe (former colonies of Britain); Algeria, Cameroon, Chad, Gabon, Ivory Coast (former colonies of France); Namibia, Togo (former colonies of Germany); Angola, Mozambique (former colonies of Portugal). This is a partial list, but enough to suggest the vast extent of western colonialism. For more extensive and specific information, consult the encyclopedia. Look up the countries on your map of Africa.

[6] Most former colonies were granted independence during the 1950s, 1960s, and 1970s. Examples-- using their current names--are Ghana: 1957; Democratic Republic of Congo, Nigeria, Togo (1960); Sierra Leone, Tanzania (1961); Algeria, Uganda (1962); Kenya (1963); Angola, Mozambique (1975). When one considers the wave of change across the continent in less than fifty years, it is not surprising that Africa continue to experience extreme growing pains.

[7] African hominids date from at least 4,000,000 years ago. Agriculture, brought in from South West Asia, appears to date from sixth or fifth millenium B.C.E. Africa's first great civilization began in Egypt in 3400 B.C.E. Ancient Ghana was already thriving from trade in gold, salt, and slaves when first recorded by Arabs in the eighth century.

[8] Eight hundred. However, they belong to relatively few language families. Since most Africans do not speak a European tongue, the use of written African languages has become increasingly important for the growing field of mass communications.

[9] Egypt. The Egyptian Coptic Church dates back to the third century and claims to have learned about Jesus from St. Mark himself. By the beginning of the fourth century, parts of the Scriptures had already been translated into several non-Greek vernacular languages of the region, and Christian churches were active throughout north Africa.

[10] This is a complex question that could provide material for a fascinating group discussion. Perhaps you have an African in your group (or could ask someone to attend) who would give his/her observations. Is it because of social-economic conditions and the response of the church? Is it because Christianity is making an appeal that is less tainted by colonialism than before? Is it because many Africans are waking up to the Christian faith just as many Western nations are becoming increasingly secular societies? Or all of the above? What other reasons come to mind?

[11] See Map'n Facts #2875

[12] See Map'n Facts #2875

[Information for answers 2 to 8, from the *Columbia Encyclopedia*, Fifth Edition, New York: Columbia University Press, 1993.]

Appendix 2

Support the International Treaty to Ban Land Mines

A Petition to the 2000 General Conference of the United Methodist Church
Sponsoring Agency: General Board of Global Ministries, The United Methodist Church

Antipersonnel land mines are weapons of mass destruction that claim the life or a limb of an innocent victim every 20 minutes. Peacekeepers, humanitarian workers, and missionaries risk death and injury daily from land mines. Today, 135 countries have signed the 1997 Mine Ban Treaty. Religious leaders, the Pope, physicians, veterans, humanitarian activists, environmentalists, and human-rights advocates have called upon the United States to sign the Mine Ban Treaty.

Antipersonnel land mines are a growing threat to the human community and the environment. They kill or maim hundreds of people every week, bring untold suffering and casualties to mostly innocent and defenseless civilians (especially children), obstruct economic development and reconstruction, inhibit the repatriation of refugees and internally displaced persons, and create other severe consequences for years after emplacement.

Therefore, the General Conference of The United Methodist Church calls upon the President of the United States and, if need be, his successor, to endorse the "Convention on the Prohibition of the Use, Stockpiling, Production and Transfer of Anti-Personnel Mines and on Their Destruction," commonly called the Mine Ban Treaty; and further, that our Council of Bishops, the General Superintendents of The United Methodist Church, send representation of that body to deliver this heartfelt call to the President as soon as possible after the adjournment of the Year 2000 General Conference.

We commit ourselves to strategies of advocacy against the deployment of land mines, de-mining and caring for persons who have been wounded by land mines.

We call upon U.S. citizens and the U.S. government to increase resources for humanitarian de-mining, mine awareness programs, and increased resources for land mine victim rehabilitation and assistance; and we ask that the Secretary of the General Conference send this resolution to the President of the United States Senate and to the Speaker of the U.S. House of Representatives as soon as possible after the adjournment of this Year 2000 General Conference.

We, the undersigned, call for an unconditional international ban on the use, production, trade, and stockpiling of landmines.

Please collect names and return to:
Church World Service
110 Maryland Ave. NE, Bldg. Box 45
Washington, DC 20002-5694

Church World Service will forward petitions to President Clinton.

Name	Signature	Address

Appendix 3
African Songs

Everybody Loves Saturday Night
Bobo Waro Ferro Satodeh

When Nigeria was a British colony, the British imposed an early evening curfew, when everyone had to be off the streets. The Nigerians protested and got the curfew lifted, at least on Saturday, the most important night of the week. This song was written to celebrate their victory and on-going defiance of the British. It has since been carried all over the world and sung in many languages. It is fun to sing in leader - chorus style.

Traditional words
Traditional folk melody
Arranged by Nylea L. Butler-Moore

LEADER FIRST, CHORUS ON REPEAT

Ev-'ry-bod-y loves Sat-ur-day night.
Boh-boh wah-roh fehr-roh Saht-oh-deh.

LEADER: Ev-'ry-bod-y, / Boh-boh wah-roh,
CHORUS: ev-'ry-bod-y, / Boh-boh wah-roh,
LEADER: ev-'ry-bod-y, / Boh-boh wah-roh,
CHORUS: ev-'ry-bod-y, / Boh-boh wah-roh,

ALL:
Ev-'ry-bod-y loves Sat-ur-day night!
Boh-boh wah-roh, fehr-roh Saht-oh-deh!

Too leh mond emm Sahmedee swar. (French)
Tout le monde aime Samedi soir.

Toedoe ell mohndoh keeair Sahbahdoe. (Spanish)
Todo el mondo quiere Sabado.

Peeach ah tootee sahbahto sairah. (Italian)
Piace a tutti sabato sera.

Vse loobyat sooboetoo vecherom. (Russian)
Ren ren seh huan lee pai loo. (Chinese)

© 1958 Cooperative Recreation Service. Transferred to World Around Songs, Inc., 20 Colbert's Creek Rd., Burnsville, NC 28714.

ANGOLA

A Kapasule

In one of the many tribal languages of Angola, *A Kapasule* means "friend" and *moi-o* means "how are you?" Some people believe that the more you sing "A Kapasule," the more your friendship will grow.

Traditional words

Traditional folk melody
Arranged by Nylea L. Butler-Moore

Ah Kah-pah-soo-leh, Ah Kah-pah-soo-leh, Ah Kah-pah-soo-leh, La la la la la la la. Moy-oh, Moy-oh, Moy-oh, Moy-oh, Moy-oh, Moy-oh, La la la la la la la.

A Ka-pa-su-le, A Ka-pa-su-le, A Ka-pa-su-le, La la la la la la la. Moi-o, Moi-o, Moi-o, Moi-o, Moi-o, Moi-o, La la la la la la la.

ZAIRE

Before Dinner

This song from the Lunda tribe of Zaire (formerly the Belgian Congo) describes the traditional duties of women and girls in preparing a meal. One girl states the task and all the others join in the chorus: "Ya, ya, ya, ya."

English words by Carol Hart Sayre

Traditional melody
Arranged by Carol Hart Sayre

Rhythmically

SOLO: First we go to hoe our gar-den, ALL: Ya, ya, ya, ya.

SOLO: Next we car-ry jugs of wa-ter, ALL: Ya, ya, ya, ya.

SOLO: Then we pound the yel-low corn, ALL: Ya, ya, ya, ya.

SOLO: Then we stir our pots of mush, ALL: Ya, ya, ya, ya.

SOLO: Now we eat—come, gath-er round the camp-fire, ALL: Ya, ya, ya, ya.

Appendix 4
African Games

Bee Hunting

Players: 12 to 20 players, ages 5 to 8, and a leader.

This is an outdoor game of daring in which young children make fun of the dangerous activity of honey gathering carried out by adults and older boys and girls in the forests of Zaire. The children need a leader who knows the rules of the game while they are learning to play it fairly. When they are able to teach new players how to be bees and hunters, they no longer need a leader.

The leader divides the players into two straight lines of bees and hunters and sends them to opposite ends of their play area. The players in each line hang on to one another by placing their right hands on the shoulder of the player ahead.

The object of the game is for the swarm of bees to "sting" the hunters by touching them with the left hand or for the hunters to surround the bees before they get back to the hive (their end of the play area). To begin, the bees buzz and move slowly in a snakelike pattern toward the hunters. The hunters pretend to look for bees in the sky and trees, moving closer to the bees all the time. When the bees begin to touch the hunters, the hunters break rank and try to surround the bees. The bees then are free to run individually to their end of the play area. Hunters who are "stung" (touched) are out of the game. Bees who are surrounded lose their "sting." Bees who return safe to their hive and hunters who have not been stung are winners.

Cock-a-doodle-do ▲

Players: rooster, rooster's parent, and hiders, ages 5 to 8
Equipment: a stick of chalk

This is an early morning Hide-and-Seek game from rural Ethiopia. The rooster's parent leads the game from a seated position; he or she might be someone who cannot run and hide.

One person draws a circle about six feet in diameter around the rooster's parent. The group decides who is going to be the first rooster. The rooster is It. It puts his or her head in the parent's lap while other players go and hide. After a short time It looks up to the parent and asks, "Cock-a-doodle-do?" The parent says, "No, the sun isn't up yet. Go back to sleep." It rests again, crows again, and finally the parent says, "Oh, the sun is up! Go look for the chicks."

It looks for the hiders. As soon as It spies one, they both race back to the parent's circle. If It gets there first, the hider is It for the next game. If the hider gets there first, he or she goes and hides again. The first hider to come in after It is always It for the next game. All other players are called to come in free after several have been caught.

Appendix 5

Recipes for an African Meal

The following recipes for a salad and a stew were supplied by Rebeccah Cobbinah (see below), who tells us that they are examples of the sort of food that would be served in average Ghanaian households.

Ghanaian Salad

1 head lettuce
2 medium tomatoes, firm and ripe (sliced into rings)
1 medium cucumber, score and sliced into thin rings
1 14 oz. can vegetarian baked beans
1 12 oz. can sweet corn (or fresh or frozen)
1 13 oz. can tuna (drain and flake)
2 cups diced or sliced carrots, fresh or frozen
4 hard-cooked eggs, sliced
1 cup snow peas (fresh or frozen)
2 large Spanish onions (thinly sliced, ring)
1/2 cup cider vinegar for marinade
1 cup mayonnaise (combine with
1/2 cup milk and blend until smooth)

Marinate sliced onion in vinegar for about thirty minutes. Slice lettuce into bite-sized pieces. In a large salad bowl, arrange alternate layers of the ingredients. Leave some egg slices for garnishing and some dressing for final topping. Store in refrigerator for 1 hour before serving. Serve with bread. May be served for breakfast or lunch. Serves 4.

Okro Stew

1 lb. okro (okro is the Ghanaian word for okra)
4 large ripe tomatoes blanched, peeled, and diced (or 14 oz. can crushed tomatoes)
2 medium eggplants, peeled and sliced
3 medium onions, finely diced
4 cloves garlic, peeled and diced
1 hot pepper, finely chopped (optional)
1 oz. dried salted fish, shredded (sold everywhere)
2 tbsp. dried powered shrimp (purchase dried shrimp; grind)

4 medium soft-shell crabs (if wrong season, use regular crabs, remove shell)
1 lb. dried beef, cut into bite-size pieces (you may substitute fresh beef: slice into strips; stir-fry)

Trim off the ends of okro and slice into thin rounds about 1/2 inch thick. In large saucepan, heat oil and saut onion until tender. Add chopped garlic and stir frequently. Add diced hot pepper, powdered shrimp, tomatoes, and salt fish. (Powdered shrimp and salt fish are used as spices or flavor enhancers; substitution of fresh products will not result in the same distinctive flavor.) Stir and let simmer for five minutes. Add okro, eggplant, and dried beef, and simmer for 30 minutes. Add crabs and simmer for 5 minutes until all ingredients are cooked and tender. Serve hot with steamed rice, banku (corn dumplings), boiled potatoes, or boiled plantains. (To make banku: Ferment corn meal for 2 days. Mix with water. Stir until thick [3045 minutes]. Shape into small dumplings. To make boiled plantains: Peel plantains and boil as you would potatoes.) Serves 4.

Rebeccah Cobbinah was born in Accra, Ghana, and has lived in the United States for the past twenty years. The mother of three children, Rebeccah is an active member of Advent Lutheran Church in Manhattan and lives in Riverdale, New York, where she runs a catering service specializing in Ghanaian and American food.

Glossary

AZT (azidothymidine). Anti-viral drug used to treat AIDS.

Borehole. Small-diameter well drilled to obtain water.

Christian Solidarity International (CSI): Swiss-based human-rights association that pays Arab traders sums of money to recover members of Sudan's Dinka tribe who have been sold into slavery.

Convention on the Rights of the Child. Adopted by the General Assembly of the UN in 1990, and premised on the conviction that children have the same full spectrum of rights as adults: civil and political, social, cultural, and economic.

Day of the African Child. Annual celebration focusing on Africa's children, with participation by schools and other civic institutions, to focus attention on the immense and continuing difficulties of Africa's children caught in the grip of ethnic and national upheavals.

FAWE (Forum for African Women Educationalists) Group of professional educators, active since 1992, that has, among other things, successfully lobbied several African countries to create a change in policies that traditionally excluded girls from school.

Global Village: Concept—not geographical location—that seeks to express the continuing interdependence and interconnectedness of human life, no matter where.

International Monetary Fund (IMF). Specialized agency of the United Nations.

Jubilee 2000: International movement, based on the biblical concept of a year of jubilee (see Lev. 25), to forgive the oppressive and crippling debt that is overwhelming many developing nations.

Lord's Resistance Army. Sudan-based paramilitary band engaged in hit-and-run tactics against Uganda, whose leader, Joseph Kony, has abducted and forced thousands of teenagers to serve as soldiers and laborers.

NGO (nongovernmental organization): An organization concerned with political and social issues that works closely with, but has no direct affiliation with, national governments.

Organization of African Unity (OAU): Organization representing Algeria, Angola, Benin, Botswana, Burkina Faso, Burundi, Cameroon, Cape Verde, Central African Republic, Chad, Comoros, Cote D'ivoire, Democratic Republic of Congo, Djibouti, Egypt, Equatorial Guinea, Eritrea, Ethiopia, Gabon, Gambia, Ghana, Guinea, Guinea-Bissau, Kenya, Lesotho, Liberia, Libya, Madagascar, Malawi, Mali, Mauritania, Mauritius, Mozambique, Namibia, Niger, Nigeria, Rwanda, Saharawi Arab Democratic Republic, Sao Tome and Principe, Seychelles, Senegal, Sierra Leone, Somalia, South Africa, Sudan,

Swaziland, Tanzania, Togo, Tunisia, Uganda, Zambia, Zimbabwe, with the purpose of promoting unity and solidarity among its members through various cooperative means.

Renamo: Resistencia Nacional Mocambicana, a Mozambican resistance movement which has been engaged in a long civil war.

Structural Adjustment. Term used to describe a major overhaul in a country's economy.

Sub-Saharan Africa. That portion of the African continent south of the Sahara desert.

UNESCO: United Nations Educational, Scientific, and Cultural Organization, a specialized agency of the UN with headquarters in Paris.

Unita. Portuguese acronym for Angolan guerrilla group, led by Jonas Savimbi, that has fought the government since Angola's independence from Portugal in 1975.

UNICEF. United Nations Children's Fund. Affiliated agency of the UN concerned with children and adolescents throughout the world, especially in devastated areas and in developing countries.

UWESO (Ugandan Women's Effort to Save Orphans). Organization founded in 1986 by Janet Museveni, wife of Ugandan president Yoweri Museveni, to save orphans created by Uganda's civil war, now focusing on AIDS orphans.

World Bank: Informal name for International Bank for Reconstruction and Development, specialized agency of the United Nations, with headquarters in Washington, DC.

World Food Program (WFP). Food aid organization of the UN.

World Health Organization (WHO) Specialized agency of the UN with headquarters in Geneva, Switzerland.

End Notes

Chapter 1

1. The State of the World's Children, 1998, UNICEF (Oxford, United Kingdom: Oxford University Press) p. 21.

2. Ibid., p. 21.

3. Ibid., p. 10.

Chapter 2

4. The State of the World's Children, 1999, UNICEF (Oxford, United Kingdom: Oxford University Press), back cover.

5. Ibid., p. 51.

6. Ibid., p. 36.

7. Ibid., p. 52.

Chapter 3

8. Mike Wessels, "Child Soldiers," Bulletin of the Atomic Scientists. November/December 1997, p. 32.

9. Robert D. Kaplan, "The Coming Anarchy," Atlantic Monthly, February 1994, pp. 44-45.

10. Graa Machel, "The Impact of Armed Conflict on Children," Document A/51/306 & Add 1, United Nations, New York, NY 10017 [Order from Public Inquiries Unit, Department of Information, United Nations, New York, NY 10017; Fax: 212-963-0071]

11. Wessels, op.cit., p. 33.

12. Michael Klare, "The Kalashinikov Age," Bulletin of the Atomic Scientists. January/February 1999, pp. 18-22.

13. Merri Rosenberg. "A Teenage Nightmare," Scholastic Update, December 8, 1997, pp. 4-6.

14. Wessels, op. cit., p. 32.

15. Klare, op. cit., pp. 18-22.

16. Kathi Austin, "Hearts of Darkness," Bulletin of the Atomic Scientists, January/February 1999, pp. 34-36.

17. Johanna McGeary and Marguerite Michaels, "Africa Rising," Time, March 30, 1998, p. 37.

Chapter 4

18. The State of the World's Children, 1997, UNICEF (Oxford, United Kingdom: Oxford University Press), p. 27.

19. The State of the World's Children, 1999, UNICEF (Oxford, United Kingdom: Oxford University Press), p. 62.

20. The State of the World's Children, 1997, UNICEF (Oxford University Press, United Kingdom), p. 30.

21. Ibid., p. 30.

22. Ibid., p. 36.

23. The State of the World's Children, 1999, UNICEF (Oxford, United Kingdom: Oxford University Press), p. 58.

24. "Child Labor," U. N. Chronicle, No. 4, 1996, p. 20.

25. "The Scourge That Won't Go Away," World Press Review, August 1998, p. 44.

26. Ibid., p. 44.

27. The Statesman Journal, Sept. 13, 1997.

28. The State of the World's Children, 1997, UNICEF (Oxford, United Kingdom: Oxford University Press), p. 9.

29. "Adjustment Lending: An Evaluation of Ten Years of Experience," UNICEF Country Economics Department. Policy and Research Series, No. 1, 1998, pp. 287-288.

30. The State of the World's Children, 1989, UNICEF, (Oxford, United Kingdom: Oxford University Press) pp. 16, 17.
31. George E. Moose. "The Economic Situation in Sub-Saharan Africa," U. S. Department of State Dispatch, August 12, 1996, Vol. 7, No. 33, p. 413.

32. "The Jubilee 2000 Campaign," Church World Service, Church World Service Home Page.

Resources

Books

ABC's (Advance Book of Children's Projects) List of more than 100 Advance ministries with children and youth. (Service Center #5173: free except for postage and handling.)

Call to Hope: Living as Christians in a Violent Society. Full-color magazine designed to help children cope with violent experiences.

Caulfield, Catherine. *Masters of Illusion: The World Bank and the Poverty of Nations.* New York: Henry Holt and Company, Inc., 1996.

Darmani, Lawrence. *African Youth Speak.* African youth speak of their lives and the issues they are most concerned about as Christians in Africa. Includes leader's guide. (Service Center #1901: $4.95 plus postage and handling.)

Lodu's Escape and Other Stories from Africa. Edited by Phoebe Mugo. (Service Center #1898: $6.95 plus postage and handling.)

Machel, Graa. *The Impact of Armed Conflict on Children, UNICEF,* 1996. [For ordering information, see Endnotes, chapter 3.]

Nordstrom, Carolyn. *Girls and War Zones: Troubling Questions.* Uppsala, Sweden: Life and Peace Institute, 1997.

The State of the World's Children, 1997, 1998, 1999, UNICEF (Oxford, United Kingdom: Oxford University Press).

Winslow, Phillip C. Sowing the Dragon's Teeth: Land Mines and the Global Legacy of War. Boston, Massachusetts: Beacon Press, 1997.

Worldwind: Mission Magazine for Children. (Service Center #2724: $1.00 plus postage and handling.)

Brochures

Africa at the Crossroads. Information about the five-year Bishops' Appeal and Campaign. (Service Center #5235: free except for postage and handling.)

Campaign for Children Continues. Summary of past actions and future struggles to continue the Campaign for Children. (Service Center #5222: free except for postage and handling.)

Children's Fund for Christian Mission. Information for children about how to contribute to selected mission projects. (Eng. Service Center #5699, Span. #1062: free except for postage and handling.)

Street Children. A bulletin insert that deals with some of the shocking facts about abandoned children living in the streets of some Latin American and African countries. Explains how local churches can help offer these children hope through Advance.

To the Least of These. This basic brochure tells the story of the compassionate ministries provided by UMCOR. Emergency Response, Refugees and World Hunger/Poverty Ministries provide the context for UMCOR's work throughout the world.

Videos

"To Love In Deed," United Methodist Women's Campaign for Children." Shows two successful outreach programs for children. (ECU Film: Rental, $10; Sale, $15)

"Why We Care . . . Africa," Twenty-six minute video about the work of the General Board of Global Ministries in response to the refugee crisis in Africa.

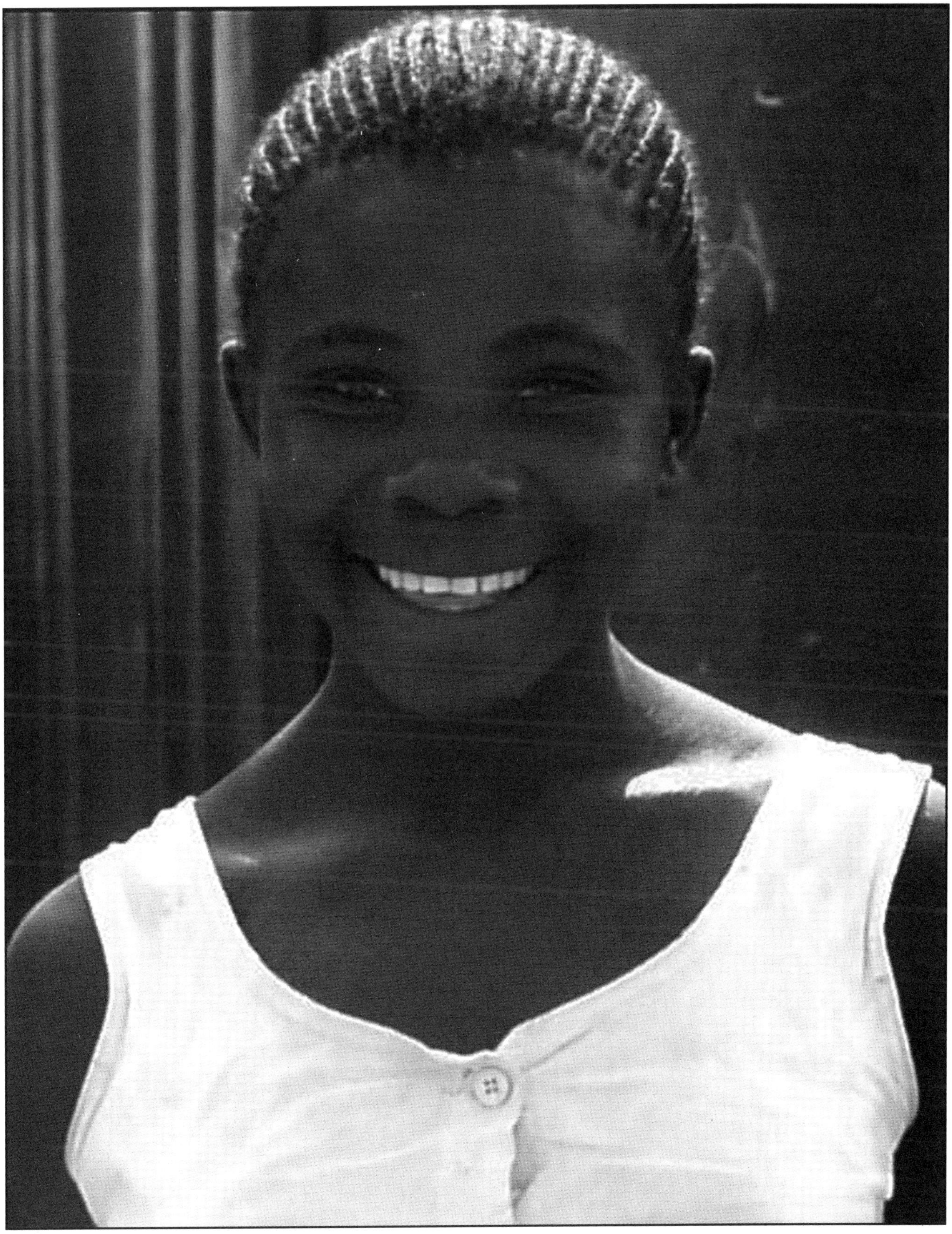

Jackie Lee Onwu is a United Methodist missionary of the General Board of Global Ministries assigned to the Grand Bahama Circuit of the Methodist Church of the Bahamas, Turks and Caicos Islands.

Her responsibilities as a member of the staff include a variety of circuit-wide ministries: development of a pre-school program at Sea Grape; establishment of after-school activities for children and youth; structuring of outreach ministries with Haitians and other minorities; assisting in development of work among the Woman & Men Program and the Home & Family Life Program; assisting in Lay Leadership Training Program at circuit and conference levels; and working with circuit and conference committees.

In addition, Jackie assists the circuit superintendent in the general administration of the Grand Bahama Circuit.

Prior to this assignment, she served from July 1995 in Jalingo, Nigeria, serving as the Educational Consultant/Facilitator for all UMCN schools and as the U.S. Embassy Liaison Officer, charged with securing visas for Nigerians who travel to the United States on Church-related business. From 1984-89 she served as a United Methodist person-in-mission teaching elementary education at the Hillcrest School in Jos, Plateau State, Nigeria.

She also served previously as a missionary in Kinshasa, Zaire (now Democratic Republic of Congo) as professor of history and English at the Institute Superior Pedagogique in its university system. She also taught research methods and critique historique at the Methodist Seminary in Wembo-Nyama, and English at the seminary's Women's School. During a period of evacuation from Zaire she taught English at the Mweya Bible College in Gitega, Burundi.

A native of Salisbury, Maryland she obtained her two degrees from Temple University in Philadelphia: a B.S. in secondary education and an M.A. in African history. She is completing a Ph.D. in third-world history.

Mrs. Onwu is married to Samuel Onwu, also assigned to the Grand Bahama Circuit as a GBGM missionary, and they have one son, Samuel Chimaobi (Putha).

Anne Leo Ellis was staff writer an director of interpretation with a division of the former Lutheran Church in America. There she helped develop a wide range of print materials dealing with multicultural ministry and other issues of social justice. She has worked as freelance editor and writer for numerous organizations, most recently the General Board of Global Ministries. Ms. Ellis compiled and edited *First We Must Listen: Living in a Multicultural Society* for Friendship Press, has published several children's books and stories, and has just completed a second children's novel. She attended Texas Lutheran College and Wartburg College, and received a Master's in English Literature from the University of Arizona. She lives in Manhattan with her spouse, William, a lawyer. They are the parents of two adult sons.

Order all resources by stock number from the Service Center.

Please mail order with check payable to:
SERVICE CENTER
P.O. BOX 691328
CINCINNATI, OH 45269-1328

COSTS FOR SHIPPING AND HANDLING:	
Sale Items:	**Free Items:**
$25 or less, add $3.50	50 or less, add $2.50
$25.01-$60, add $4.50	51-400, add $3.50
$60.01-$100, add $5.50	Over 400, add 75¢ per 100
Over $100, add 5%	

For billed or credit card orders
CALL TOLL FREE: 1-800-305-9857 FAX ORDERS: 1-513-761-3722
If billing is requested, $1.50 billing fee is charged.
Mail to: SERVICE CENTER, GENERAL BOARD OF GLOBAL MINISTRIES,
THE UNITED METHODIST CHURCH, 7820 READING RD. CALLER NO. 1800
CINCINNATI, OH 45222-1800

Price: $6.95   chlorine free   Stock #2860